⚏B The Practitioner's Bookshelf

*Hands-On Language and Literacy Books for
Classroom Teachers and Administrators*

DOROTHY S. STRICKLAND,
Founding Editor, Language and Literacy Series
CELIA GENISHI AND DONNA E. ALVERMANN,
*Language and Literacy Series Editors**

** For a list of current titles in the Lar ⋯ ⋯ ⋯ ⋯ ⋯ ⋯ ⋯m*

D1091381

Keep Them Reading

An Anti-Censorship Handbook for Educators

ReLeah Cossett Lent
Gloria Pipkin

Foreword by Pat Scales

Teachers College, Columbia University
New York and London

Published by Teachers College Press, 1234 Amsterdam Avenue, New York, NY 10027

Photographs in Chapter 3 by Robin Shader
Figures 3.2 and 4.1–4.6 are available as free printable downloads on TCPress.com

Library of Congress Cataloging-in-Publication Data

Lent, ReLeah Cossett.
  Keep them reading : an anti-censorship handbook for educators / ReLeah Cossett Lent,
    Gloria Pipkin.
      p. cm. — (The practitioner's bookshelf)
  Includes bibliographical references and index.
  ISBN 978-0-8077-5378-1 (pbk. : alk. paper)
  ISBN 978-0-8077-5388-0 (hardcover : alk. paper)
    1. Academic freedom—United States. 2. Teaching, Freedom of—United States.
  3. Textbooks—Censorship—United States. 4. Public schools—Curricula—Censorship—
  United States. I. Pipkin, Gloria. II. Title.
  LC72.2.L46 2012
  378.1′213—dc23   2012024769

ISBN 978-0-8077-5378-1 (paper)
ISBN 978-0-8077-5388-0 (hardcover)

Printed on acid-free paper
Manufactured in the United States of America

20 19 18 17 16 15 14 13   8 7 6 5 4 3 2 1

Contents

Foreword

ON JUNE 25, 2012, at the annual conference of the American Library Association, the Freedom to Read Foundation sponsored a special event with Stephen Chbosky, the author of *The Perks of Being a Wallflower*. Chbosky arranged for the group to preview the film based on his novel, and afterward he entertained questions about the impact his book has had on young adult readers and what it was like to direct a film of his own creation. This was indeed an exceptional opportunity for free speech advocates, but there was something else worthy of celebration on this day. Exactly 30 years ago the Supreme Court handed down the decision on the landmark *Board of Education* v. *Pico* case. This decision declared, "Local public school boards cannot ban books from school libraries merely because they dislike the ideas expressed in them." *Pico* remains the precedent case that grants young adults the right to borrow books such as *The Perks of Being a Wallflower* from their school libraries. Unfortunately the same law that gives them the "right" to read the novel doesn't give them the "right" to study it. Novels like *The Perks of Being a Wallflower* still pit teachers against the censors, and the losers of these battles are the students.

In some ways I would love being a high school student today. There are so many good novels taught in the curriculum, including contemporary young adult novels that allow readers to make the important connection between life and literature. But here's the dark reality: Too many teachers feel threatened by the censors—and by school boards that want to avoid any type of controversy—that they feel it's better to "play it safe." Is it possible to avoid controversy in the current political environment? How do the Internet and cable news advance the agenda of would-be censors? What happens when teachers come face to face with the "dark forces" of an uninformed community?

There are no easy answers, but there are lessons to be learned from the "good fight" of classroom teachers who have been victims of the censorship wars. Many have battle scars, and they deserve medals for their personal valor. *Keep Them Reading: An Anti-Censorship Handbook for Educators* offers sage advice and guidance about what to do when the censor calls.

How enlightened students must feel when they are in the classroom of a brave English teacher who believes that students have the capacity to see in a work of literature what the censors are incapable of seeing.

—Pat Scales, author of
Teaching Banned Books: 12 Guides for Young Readers

Acknowledgments

THE ISSUES in this book are close to our hearts, and we are deeply grateful to those who have helped us in this endeavor, specifically the authors and experts who lent their voices to Chapter 8 in support of the freedom to read: Judy Blume, Chris Crutcher, Jimmy Santiago Baca, Julie Anne Peters, Lauren Myracle, Lisa Luedeke, Joan Bertin, Millie Davis, Joan Kaywell, Teri Lesesne, David Moshman, and Fredonia Ray. We are also indebted to Pat Scales for her ongoing work against censorship and for writing our Foreword.

The professionals at Teachers College Press made our job easy. Meg Lemke worked with us early on in shaping the manuscript and Emily Spangler offered valuable advice as we continued the project, as did Karl Nyberg, our impressive production editor. We are thrilled with both the cover design and chapter-opening images that Dave Strauss created, and we appreciate the time and effort that he spent to help make this a visually compelling book.

We also want to express our gratitude and love to ReLeah's husband, Bert, and her father, Don Cossett, who read each chapter as it was written and offered valuable suggestions.

This book is dedicated to the many students, educators, authors, and countless others who care about intellectual freedom and work in countless ways to oppose censorship—and keep our students reading.

Introduction

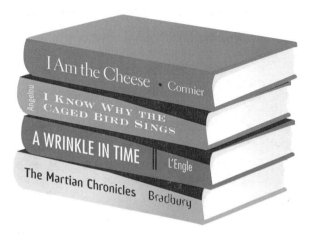

MUCH OF WHAT we've learned about censorship grew out of our experiences as colleagues in a middle school English department in northwest Florida during the 1980s. In *At the Schoolhouse Gate: Lessons in Intellectual Freedom* (Pipkin & Lent, 2002), we chronicled those experiences (both positive and negative) in hopes that we might inform, inspire, and equip other teachers who seek to instill a lifelong love of reading in their students.

Our journey began when, as a department, we decided that powerful and engaging young adult literature was the means by which we would address our curriculum. We provided a wide range of choices for independent reading, time to read in class, and opportunities for students to reflect on their reading through journal entries and responses from their teachers as well as informal discussions with other readers.

We were aware of the possibility of challenges to some of the books we used, so at Open House each fall, we emphasized to parents the value of self-selected reading, invited them to read with their children, and respond in writing, just as our students did. Most of all, we wanted them to understand that no student was required to read *any* particular book.

With works that had been selected for whole-class reading, we offered alternates to families who asked for them. Such requests for other choices were rare, but they were always honored. Although our critics suggested that any student who chose an alternative book would be teased or even ostracized, we were never aware of any evidence to support such a claim. Gloria once asked a class if they knew that one reader had substituted (with permission) another book for the one the class read, studied, and discussed, but no one had noticed. Our students instinctively accepted and honored the right of individuals to make such choices for themselves.

ADDRESSING CONCERNS AND COMPLAINTS

We mistakenly believed that because our department had been recognized by the National Council of Teachers of English as one of 150 Centers of Excellence in the country, parents would trust us to select appropriate curricular materials for their children. We began to hear that some parents were concerned about the books in our classroom libraries, however, as well as some we had selected for whole-class reading and study. Our response emphasized our commitment to honoring family standards and individual requests. We also adopted policies that allowed alternative book selections for whole-class reading and offered copies of class novels for parents to read and judge for themselves. In attempting to create a culture of reading, we invited families to attend an evening session to discuss our reading program.

FORMAL CHALLENGES

Even with our continuing efforts to communicate with parents and to respect their choices of books for their children, we received two formal complaints. The targeted books were Robert Cormier's *I Am the Cheese* (2007) and Susan Beth Pfeffer's *About David* (1980). Both complaints originated with the same parent, who then convinced other parents that they should look more closely at the "inappropriate" books being offered to students. Cormier's young adult classic deals with a family betrayed by their own government, and Pfeffer's book opens with the main character trying to understand why her best friend shot and killed his parents and then took his own life. The complaint regarding *I Am the Cheese* focused on the following three issues:

- vulgar language
- depressing content
- inappropriate sexual content

The complaint regarding *About David* centered on what the parent deemed as the teachers' lack of training and experience in addressing suicide.

At first it looked as though the superintendent intended to ban these books outright, but he finally agreed to organize a review committee to make a recommendation. We were relieved when the committee recommended that both challenged books remain in the curriculum. Almost immediately, however, the superintendent rejected their findings and developed his own plan for creating committees to review instructional materials from all secondary schools. His ruling removed all supplemental books as well as literature textbooks from classroom use until teachers could write rationales for each of them and categorize them according to the amount of sex or profanity they contained. ReLeah described this incredible situation as "the grand censoring of everything."

MEDIA ATTENTION

While our local newspaper provided front-page coverage of the unfolding censorship saga, our chief critic purchased half-page ads featuring controversial excerpts from award-winning fiction for adolescents. Letters to the editor began to sizzle, but some of the most inspired letters were from our students who wrote eloquently about the books they loved and the importance of having a wide range of reading choices.

In addition to local media coverage of the censorship issue, Peter Carlson (1987), a reporter for *The Washington Post*, made two visits to our hometown. He interviewed teachers and their critics, attended school board meetings, and wrote a major story for *The Post*'s Sunday magazine ("Banning Books in the Schools: When Teachers and Fundamentalists Clash, Children Get Burned") that featured a cover photo of *I Am the Cheese* in flames. The *St. Petersburg Times* (now the *Tampa Bay Times*) reprinted the *Post* article, and a wave of letters poured in, nearly all of them supportive. Later that year, *The Orlando Sentinel* used its own Sunday magazine cover to highlight "Profiles in Courage" and to feature one of our students, Joe Ganakos, the founder of S.A.V.E., Students Against the Violation of Education. At one point, Gloria even had reporters from Swedish radio and television in her living room.

COMMUNITY SUPPORT

Local supporters who wanted to offer encouragement began sending flowers to each of us as a show of solidarity, and we also received letters from teachers and students at other schools. The principal from one of the high schools spoke out against the ongoing censorship and encouraged his English department as they joined us to save the books that had now been effectively banned from use in their own school.

A local organization also formed to support teachers and books under fire and called themselves the Bay Educational Forum (BEF), chaired by the director of the Bay County public library. One of the most valuable contributions of BEF was a series of book discussions called "A Family Reading Experience," which began with an introduction to Young Adult literature led by Gloria and a number of her students. The highlight of the series was the personal appearance of author Robert Cormier, who joined ReLeah in leading a discussion of his book *I Am the Cheese*. At the conclusion of the packed session, one of our major critics approached Cormier and shook his hand, clearly disarmed by this gentle man whose work he had vilified.

LINES IN THE SAND

With increased media attention, the controversy escalated and both sides of the issue became even more entrenched. Churches joined the battle, passing out petitions against the books for their congregations to sign. Three teachers (including Gloria, ReLeah, and Alyne Farrell, the teacher who taught *About David*) as well as the local television reporter who was covering the events—and offering editorials against censorship—received a death threat letter. School board meetings were soon overflowing not only with local citizens but with others from out of town such as professors from nearby Florida State University. The superintendent refused to budge, and organizations including the National Coalition Against Censorship and the National Council of Teachers of English came forward to weigh in.

The superintendent ultimately relented on his order for all books to be categorized according to the degree of "inappropriateness" only after the mayor intervened, unhappy about the recent international press that identified Panama City, Florida, as "The Town that Banned Shakespeare." He and other city officials feared the loss of tourism and future business if the matter wasn't resolved. It took a lawsuit, however, to restore *I Am the Cheese* and *About David* to the curriculum.

LEGAL ACTION

As veterans of extended struggles that spanned over 2 decades, we saw exemplary literacy programs and an award-winning student newspaper sponsored by ReLeah decimated due to censorship. Our battles leave us with mixed feelings about the value of legal action. Although we will remain eternally grateful to the attorneys who represented us and the cause we hold dear, we were naïve in believing that the courts would provide "justice." We were also not prepared for the legal complexities that took months of our lives and left us with an unvarnished view of the legal system, which can be more unsettling than reassuring. As Nilsen and Donelson, authors of *Literature for Today's Young Adults* (2009), point out, most censorship cases do not result in legal hearings or court decisions but are, instead, heard in the court of public opinion. Court cases are expensive and traumatic and often serve to divide communities and faculties.

GOING FORWARD

We are often hesitant to share the most egregious particulars of our story because we don't want to scare anyone into allowing censorship to go unchecked in an effort to avoid what happened to us. Alas, if we had known then what we know now, we might have been able to avoid much pain on both sides of the issue. That was then, however, and we want to focus on *now*. We offer our experience, along with some sound advice and pertinent research, in the hope that we may help others deal with challenges and censorship in a reasoned manner.

We ask our readers to share in our quest for understanding intellectual freedom and ensuring its safety whenever possible. We have published articles in journals on the topic, keynoted at conferences, and have been honored at gatherings of like-minded people. Gloria was director of the Florida Coalition Against Censorship for several years and ReLeah is now chair of NCTE's Standing Committee Against Censorship. It seemed a natural next step that we would put what we have learned into a book that would help others deal with this complex and frustrating topic.

PREPARING FOR THE STORM

In the chapters that follow, we first look at the importance of reading, because censorship is really a moot point if we aren't committed to the idea that reading matters, perhaps more than anything else we do in our classrooms. We then explore the full meaning of censorship (and challenges), ferreting out the intricacies that define it, along with a surprising look at what has been challenged/censored in the past and why. We also consider different types of censorship as a way of expanding our understanding.

Chapter 3 provides engaging activities and simulations that can be used in the classroom as well as within the community to help all parties view challenges from varied perspectives in a thoughtful manner. We then offer a plan of action with examples of district policies regarding challenged materials, rationales for using works with whole classes, sample letters to parents about the value of classroom libraries, and other organizational tools that will help preempt a challenge rather than only resisting it once it happens.

Finally, we argue that schools and districts should take the necessary precautions for a challenge well in advance of the event. A district-level literacy coach told ReLeah recently that their district didn't really need a policy for challenged materials because they "hadn't had any incidents" and if one occurred, she trusted the school board to "do the right thing." We are dismayed when we hear what we consider to be a naïve response to such a potentially volatile issue. Teachers, administrators, district staff, superintendents, school boards, and even preservice teachers who have yet to develop a single lesson plan would do well to think through and discuss with one another the issues presented in this book. Once a challenge emerges, emotions inevitably up the ante, and it may then become impossible to create some sort of policy that will satisfactorily deal with the problem. Consider it analogous to making a plan for evacuation in case of a hurricane or following a plan for safety if a tornado is sighted. When the storm is on our doorstep we can't think clearly, but we *can* follow the procedures we established when the skies were clear.

LOOKING FOR THE LIGHT

We offer this book, then, so that others may learn from our experiences, avoid our mistakes, and take hope in our successes. In our case, we felt we had no choice but to oppose censorship with all we could muster, and we know many teachers feel the same, while desperately wanting to avoid the often public confrontation. This book is our best attempt to uphold the tenets of intellectual freedom while still honoring the values of individual students and families. It is our fervent desire that such issues can be handled with diplomacy rather than with war, and in this book we have provided the tools for diplomatic action while still opposing censorship in all its forms.

Long ago we looked to Dylan Thomas for inspiration and courage, and as we wrote the chapters of this book—seeking balance between understanding the motive of censors and the determination to ensure the rights of readers—we found ourselves returning to his poem "Do Not Go Gentle Into That Good Night." Taking the risks that make our lives meaningful can be chilling and challenging, but our experience will always tell us to "rage, rage against the dying of the light," whatever its source.

CHAPTER I

Why Reading Matters

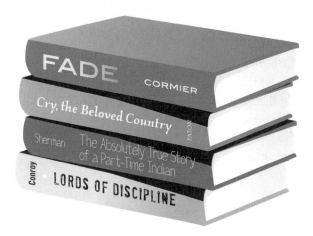

WHEN ReLEAH FACILITATES literacy workshops for teachers and administrators, she begins with a simple question: "What have you read recently that you are dying to share with us?" More often than not, the room ignites as teachers say things like, "You *have* to read *State of Wonder*" (Patchett, 2011) or "This is an older book, but I just re-discovered it and I can't stop thinking about it. It's *The Sunflower*" (Wiesenthal, 1998). A social studies teacher offered a historical novel, *Caleb's Crossing* (Brooks, 2011). "It's good," he said, "but it makes me so *angry*." He talked about how we often know the endings of such books but it doesn't ease the pain or make us regret any less what happened in the past. Perhaps one of the most profound comments came from a teacher in Massachusetts who said she was reading *Let the Great World Spin* (McCann, 2009) and then added softly, "Reading reminds me to love myself."

These conversations are not about curriculum or "best practices." They are about our reading lives. Now, perhaps more than at any time in the past, we must balance "informational text" with books that allow students to experience events that may mirror their own or, conversely, open up vast landscapes they didn't know existed.

The amazing thing about reading is that it is a different experience for each person based upon his or her individual traumas, epiphanies, beliefs, and worldviews. Louise Rosenblatt's reader-response theory argues that a reader brings to the text his or her own interpretation and aesthetic reaction (Rosenblatt, 1994). This reaction is an emotional experience that creates strong, often lifelong bonds between reader and text.

We experience these bonds when certain books stay with us forever, causing us to name our children after one of the characters or reducing us to heaving lumps of emotions. And we appreciate how reading is individualized beyond reason when a book brings us to heights of understanding, such as *Cry the Beloved Country* (Paton, 2003) did for ReLeah when she read it for the first time, or as *The Collected Sonnets of Edna St. Vincent Millay* (1988) did for Gloria when she discovered it as a young girl. Yet when we recommend these books to others, some read a few pages and say, "I don't think this is for me."

Christine Jenkins's research on "reading effects" (2008) found that content does not predict how readers will respond to the text. "Readers respond to and are affected by texts in ways specific to each reader in the context of a particular time and place. This means that even the same book may have different effects on the same reader under different circumstances" (p. 233). Jenkins noted that the perspective each reader brings to the text is informed by the reader's "personality, gender, education, age, reading ability, and other characteristics" (p. 233).

As much as policymakers want to standardize reading and reduce it to a formula that can be packaged and sold in programs or textbook series, it always slips away, eluding and taunting them as cleverly as the little gingerbread boy. The reason is that reading, especially fiction, is not a singular, objective experience; we complex human beings bring to the text all that we are and hope to be.

Nancie Atwell, in her inspiring book *The Reading Zone: How to Help Kids Become Skilled, Passionate, Habitual, Critical Readers* (2007), writes, "Every day they [kids] engage with literature that enables them to know things, feel things, imagine things, hope for things, become people they never could have dreamed without the transforming power of books, books, books" (p. 19).

If for no other reason, we must ensure that a wide variety of books is available to our students so that they have every opportunity to find that one book that can change them in ways that we may never be able to quantify. We don't know which book that might be, so the best we can do is offer up a smorgasbord of titles from which kids can choose in an effort to meet their intellectual, educational, and emotional needs.

THE RESEARCH ABOUT READING

While we are content to have kids read because we know reading has the capacity for altering their lives, we suspect that others may see reading as the means to higher test scores or decreased dropout rates. We can come together in our goals, however, if we all agree that the more kids read, the better readers they will become. While it seems unnecessary to cite research that shows just that, we want to make this point clear. Let's begin with a segment in *Education Week Classroom Q & A* with Larry Ferlazzo (2012), where he poses this question to a panel of reading practitioners, writers, researchers, and professors: "What is the best advice you would give to teachers trying to help their students become better readers?" In a three-part series, he allows these experts, many of whom have been working in this area for decades, to answer the question. What do all of their responses have in common? Take a look:

- Stephen Krashen, emeritus professor of education at the University of Southern California and the author of *The Power of Reading* (2004), answers the question simply: "Provide access to reading material, through classroom and school libraries. This is of crucial importance for those with little access to books at home and in their communities."
- Richard Allington, professor of literacy studies at the University of Tennessee and author of *What Really Matters to Struggling Readers: Designing Research-Based Programs* (2011) is equally to-the-point: "All students need to engage in lots of reading every school day. Most of this reading should be self-selected reading. Skip the worksheets, skip the low-level interrogations, and provide the time to read and the books that kids want to read and can read."
- Nancie Atwell, internationally known educator, author, and consultant, says, "No child who didn't read a lot ever became a strong reader. Building a classroom library of compelling, young adult titles is a place to begin."
- Cris Tovani, author of *I Read It But I Don't Get It: Comprehension Strategies for Adolescent Readers* (2000) as well as many other articles and books about adolescent reading, offers succinct, common sense: "People who read well, read often."
- Regie Routman, reading teacher for over 40 years, international reading consultant, and author of *Reading Essentials: The Specifics You Need to Teach Reading Well* (2002) says, "Once students have the '"right"' book, they must have uninterrupted time to read it.

Sustained time to read continuous, meaningful texts, most of which are self-selected, must be the mainstay of any reading program. While shared reading and guided reading are important teaching scaffolds to support students' move to independence, without daily, independent practice time, carefully monitored—mostly through one-on-one conferences—students are not likely to become fluent, comprehending readers."

- Laura Robb, teacher, consultant, and author of 18 books about literacy, offers the following advice: "My hope is that teachers will build class libraries with 700 to 1,000 books and magazines on a wide range of topics and reading levels."
- Kylene Beers, author of several books and articles about reading, including the bestselling *When Kids Can't Read, What Teachers Can Do* (2003), takes a proactive stance to this issue: "Stand in your principal's office every day asking that he figure out how to get more books of varying difficulty into your classroom."

That's only a sampling of views from experts about reading. Gay Ivey has also looked at reading extensively in her work. She says that giving students books that encompass a variety of formats and genres is non-negotiable if we really want struggling readers to improve (2011). Ivey and Fisher summarize the research nicely by writing, "Wide independent reading develops fluency, builds vocabulary and knowledge of text structures, and offers readers the experiences they need to read and construct meaning with more challenging texts" (2006, p. 120). And, if you want to talk standardized tests, take a look at a study conducted by Anderson, Wilson, and Fielding (1988) that found a strong correlation between the time students spend reading and their scores on standardized tests.

Even the Common Core State Standards, with which we have major concerns, recognize the importance of wide and frequent reading. The document "Publishers Criteria for Common Core Standards" states,

Additional materials markedly increase the opportunity for regular independent reading of texts that appeal to students' interests to develop both their knowledge and joy in reading. These materials should ensure that all students have daily opportunities to read texts of their choice on their own during and outside of the school day. Students need access to a wide range of materials on a variety of topics and genres both in their classrooms and in their school libraries to ensure that they have opportunities to independently read broadly and widely to build their knowledge, experience, and joy in reading. (Coleman & Pimentel, 2011, p. 4)

CLASSROOM LIBRARIES

When these authors, researchers, and teachers talk about students having ready access to a wide variety of texts from various genres, they are talking about classroom libraries. The Alliance of Excellent Education, International Reading Association, and National Council of Teachers of English are only a few of many large educational organizations that also advocate the use of classroom libraries. With such libraries, students have access to books and other resources at their fingertips. Pilgreen (2000) notes that in successful reading programs, the burden of finding books does not rest on the students. The teacher should ensure that all students find something interesting they can read.

Classroom libraries contain materials that are not generally texts adopted by the state boards of education. Such collections are created by the teacher and/or students to meet their interests and needs. Often teachers, especially English teachers, will begin the process by bringing in books that they have already collected and then supplementing those with additional titles as they go along. Think of classroom libraries as you would school or public libraries, only on a smaller scale. Magazines, graphic novels, student publications, poetry, fiction, and nonfiction are samples of what may be found in a classroom library. In this digital age, classroom libraries have expanded with the use of iPads and laptops. Simon and Schuster, for example, sponsors a site where 14–18-year-old students can register, read new YA books online (for free), and post reviews about them.

How to Create a Classroom Library

Following are ways to establish a classroom library:

1. Especially when you are first creating a classroom library, check out books from your school library on a certain topic or have the media specialist gather a variety of books that students might enjoy, such as those recommended at www.teenreads.com, a site that offers books reviews, author profiles, and best books for teens.
2. Look for bargain books online as well as in bookstores. Pick up your educator discount card at Books-a-Million or Barnes and Noble and head for their bargain department. We have found great YA books priced at 1 dollar each at Books-a-Million. Recently, by using our discount we walked out of the store with a whole sack full of books for a cost of only 80 cents each.

3. Tell students, parents, and other teachers what types of books you are seeking. We have had students donate current, popular books that they had read and were ready to give away.

4. Take Kylene Beers's advice and go straight to your principal or team leader. Armed with the research in this chapter, tell her that you *must* get your kids reading and you need books. Look for mini-grants or approach your school advisory committee; they will often offer funding for projects based on the school improvement plan. And what school improvement plan doesn't focus on reading?

Choosing Books for Classroom Libraries

ReLeah once heard a consultant say that teachers should not place any book in their classroom library that they had not personally read. In a perfect world that might be good advice, but considering how busy teachers are, this rule would ensure very slim classroom libraries. Since classroom libraries are, in effect, extensions of school libraries, the same guidelines should govern both—and we all know that librarians can't read every book they place on their shelves. In most districts, all that is required is that the classroom teacher keep a current inventory of the books in her library. Other districts ask that the teacher provide a list of her books to the media specialist, who will keep them on file. Note that it is not the media specialist's job to approve the list, merely to house it with her own inventory of books. Student class librarians can take care of creating classroom library inventories as well as facilitating the checkout process.

Award-Winning Books

As you choose books, look for award-winning titles. The following sites will help in your search.

- The Young Adult library Services Association provides a list of awards (and booklists) at www.ala.org/yalsa/booklistsawards/booklistsbook. Pay particular attention to the Printz Awards for Excellence in Young Adult Literature (www.ala.org/yalsa/printz). You will also find lists of "quick picks for reluctant readers," "outstanding books for college bound," and "best books written for teens."
- The National Book Foundation now gives a National Book Award in the category of "young people's literature." We have found these

books to be well-written as well as appealing to teens. Go to www. nationalbook.org/nba2011.html for a list.

- The Coretta Scott King award, sponsored by the American Library Association, is given to African American authors and illustrators. The titles promote understanding and appreciation of the culture of all peoples. Find the list at www.ala.org/emiert/cskbookawards.
- For nonfiction, go to www.ncte.org/awards/orbispictus and find a list of books honored for their excellence. This award is sponsored by the National Council of Teachers of English.

To some extent, these awards act as a type of security blanket, but we must remember that, much like Linus's blanket, it only offers imagined security. Award-winning books can be challenged as readily as any other book, but it will help to show that experts in the field acknowledge the book as a worthy read.

The most glaring example of an award-winning book being censored is Sherman Alexie's *The Absolutely True Diary of a Part-Time Indian* (2008), which was winner of the National Book Award and was on the *New York Times* bestseller list. The American Library Association's Office of Intellectual Freedom (OIF) spotlighted this book in their OIF Blog (www.oif. ala.org/oif/?p=1500), and detailed the challenges. Sherman Alexie made this statement on the blog: "I believe censorship is really about condescension. It's the notion that kids don't have complicated emotional lives, don't have complicated responses to a complicated life. Censorship is an attempt to make kids and their lives simple." While we can't agree with censorship in any form, as optimists we can see a silver lining as censored authors talk about why their books are important and create a discussion that may bring both sides closer together. See Chapter 3 for ideas about creating school and community-wide forums on censorship and intellectual freedom.

ADVANTAGES OF STUDENT-SELECTED READING

One of the reasons that we advocate classroom libraries and time for independent reading is that such activities tap into an essential factor of engagement: choice. According to Brian Cambourne, head of the Centre for Studies in Literacy at Wollongong University in Australia, learners should be allowed to make choices about "when, how and what 'bits' to learn" as a condition of engagement in learning (1995). Other researchers also acknowledge the importance of choice in reading achievement. John Guthrie in *Engaging Adolescents in Reading* (2008), for example, lists "control and choice" as one of three essential factors in creating motivated, engaged readers (p. 10).

The Common Core State Standards also advocate having students read a wide variety of increasingly complex texts. Calkins, Ehrenworth, and Lehman argue in their book *Pathways to the Common Core: Accelerating Achievement* (2012) that a critical part of this goal is "provisioning students with an extensive collection of high-interest accessible books" and providing choice over what students will read (p. 50).

In addition, there is research that links choice to increased comprehension. Allington and Gabriel make the point that "The research base on student-selected reading is robust and conclusive. Students read more and understand more and are more likely to continue reading when they have the opportunity to choose what they read" (2012, p. 10). Also inherent in student choice are intrinsic rewards that lead to self-efficacy and a sense of personal responsibility.

Lois Lowry, multi-award-winning author of many young adult books, including the famous and oft-censored *The Giver* (2011), may provide the best reason for providing students with choice. "I believe without a single shadow of a doubt that it is necessary for young people to learn to make choices. Learning to make right choices is the only way they will survive in an increasingly frightening world. Pretending that there are no choices to be made—reading only books, for example, which are cheery and safe and nice—is a prescription for disaster for the young" (p. 55).

Choice May Preempt Censorship

Choice is a great diffuser of censorship as well. When every student in a class is assigned the same novel or text, chances are much greater that a challenge will emerge than when students are allowed to make decisions regarding their own reading, especially if they are encouraged to confer with their parents about their choices. Even if students choose one novel from several that the teacher has selected, say for literature circles, they are making decisions that place them in charge of their own reading. These choices mean that they, rather than their teacher, should answer for those decisions.

When ReLeah was teaching an 11th-grade English class, for example, one of her students chose Robert Cormier's novel *Fade* (1988) from the classroom library. She was surprised when the student's mother asked for a conference regarding the appropriateness of the novel. ReLeah insisted that the student be present at the meeting since only he could explain his reasons for checking out the book. The parent began the meeting by saying that she had discovered the book in her son's room and, upon flipping through the pages of the novel, had found some of the scenes "shocking," particularly those relating to an incident of incest. "We don't want our son reading about incest," she said calmly. Turning to the student, ReLeah asked if he found the scenes offensive and if he felt he had violated his family's values by reading the book. The ensuing discussion between mother and son left ReLeah as an observer. Instead of asking why ReLeah permitted her son to read the book, the mother asked her son why *he* was reading the book. His honest answer, that he hadn't given the scene much thought because he was so taken with the idea that someone could become invisible, allayed the mother's fears and diffused a potentially volatile situation.

While every challenge may not end so positively, it is important to tell students at the beginning of the year that they, not the teacher, must defend their reading choices and ensure that they are adhering to their own family's standards. The teacher's responsibility is to provide a wide range of developmentally appropriate titles for her grade level.

Literature Circles vs. Whole-Class Novels

We advocate the use of literature circles or small-group reading whenever possible for a variety of reasons. The most important reason is that when students have opportunities to talk about what they are reading and learning in small groups, their comprehension and cognitive skills increase (Harvey & Daniels, 2009). Calkins, Ehrenworth, and Lehman agree; they state, "If your goal is to accelerate readers' ability to comprehend increasingly complex texts, matching readers to books is necessary, but not sufficient. The engine that motors readers' development is the time spent in engaged reading and in talking and writing about that reading" (2012, p. 52). The other reason, as we discussed earlier, is that assigning one novel to everyone in the class is like waving a red flag in the faces of would-be censors.

If you must use whole-class novels, we can't emphasize strongly enough the necessity of providing an alternate selection. Unfortunately, even that reasonable step is often not enough. In our own censorship case, ReLeah's 7th-grade student was offered an alternative chosen by her mother, but then the parent had additional objections. First, she contended that the novel in question (*I Am the Cheese*) was not appropriate for *any* student, and second, she insisted that her daughter would be ostracized if she had to read a novel that differed from the one her classmates studied. We have often wondered if our life-altering censorship event would not have happened had the student in question been part of a literature circle reading a book with a small group of her peers who had also *chosen* that same book.

In short, if you want to minimize challenges, engage students in independent reading or literature circles where students choose a book out of several that meet your teaching objectives. If you do choose to teach one novel to the entire class, provide several alternate selections.

READING AND THE COMMON CORE STANDARDS

As we noted earlier, the Common Core State Standards insist that students read "complex texts," and while we can't argue with the premise that one of the functions of school is to teach students how to approach challenging text, we are concerned that teachers will be relegated to giving every student in a class a common, difficult, uninteresting text that they can't or won't read—leading to an even further decline in reading. We advocate providing appealing texts on the ability levels of our students and then scaffolding their reading skills through increasingly challenging and *interesting* texts—with choice as a major component. Richard Allington makes this case in an article entitled "You Can't Learn Much from Books You Can't Read" (2002). In a later article, he continues the argument by explaining, "Sadly, struggling readers typically encounter a steady diet of too-challenging texts throughout the school day as they make their way through classes that present grade-level material hour after hour. In essence, traditional instructional practices widen the gap between readers" (Allington & Gabriel, 2012, p. 12).

Thomas Newkirk notes that most excellent nonfiction involves narrative, and that we should be teaching students how that structure works in their reading. He contends that "so-called 'informational texts' work only when the writer has been able to establish a set of expectations to drive the reading. Otherwise, there is no motor, no dynamic forward movement" (2012, p. 32). He contends that giving readers nonfiction for the purpose of learning bits of information will eventually defeat them.

As odd as it sounds, perhaps our greatest fear is that challenges and censorship of books in school will completely disappear with the adoption of the Common Core State Standards because students, especially in the upper grades, will not be reading much fiction at all in the quest for "informational" and "complex text." And when they do read fiction, it will only be "challenging" classics. As a high school English teacher told Re-Leah when she asked her what young adult novels her students were reading, "We're not really reading YA fiction anymore—the Common Core, you know. I have to teach them how to read the hard stuff."

Reading only the hard stuff, the "glorified phone book" (Newkirk, 2012) of informational texts, will not instill a love of reading nor will it help students become better readers. Unfortunately, it won't even meet the goals that the creators of the Common Core State Standards seek, to improve our standing among all developed countries in literacy. What it will take, as researchers have repeatedly shown, is to make reading accessible and enjoyable.

FOR THE LOVE OF BOOKS

If you love books, as we do, Pat Conroy's *My Reading Life* (2010) will be a homecoming for you. He writes,

> I read for fire. I have done so since the day I read *Look Homeward, Angel* (Wolfe, 1995). Now, at last, I know what I was looking for then. I wanted to be lit up, all the cities and all the hill towns within me sacked and torn to the ground and the crops destroyed and the earth salted. Now, when I pick up a book, the prayer that rises out of me is that it changes me utterly and that I am not the man who first selected that book from a well-stocked shelf. (p. 243)

Look Homeward, Angel may not be the book that sets your students on fire, but they will never find the book that does unless we offer them choices and more choices, unless we show them the treasures hidden within the covers of a book or the screens of their iPad or electronic reader. Perhaps more than any other responsibility we have as teachers, we must help our students experience the inevitable transformation that occurs through reading, and we must do everything we can to offer and then protect the book that just might change their lives.

Understanding Challenges and Censorship

C ENSORSHIP IS NOT an easy concept to grasp because it comes in so many different forms, some of which may not easily be recognized. If the government took books from a school and burned them in the courtyard, there would be no end to the protests of such a blatant act of censorship. When books by Jimmy Santiago Baca, Sandra Cisneros, Junot Diaz, and Matt de la Pena, to name only a few authors, were boxed up, taken out of schools, and put into storage in Tucson, Arizona, after Mexican American Studies Programs were discontinued, the act was decried as censorship by some, but generally reported and then ignored by the mainstream press.

Censorship, much like words such as *patriotism*, has shades of meaning, depending upon the perspective of the user. One person sees censorship as a violation of our most fundamental rights; to another it is simply a selection of one book over another, and to still another it is a way of protecting children from perceived evil ideas. Despite these differences, most people do not want to be accused of censorship and, in fact, vehemently deny they are participating in it, using euphemisms (such as "rating a book" or "restructuring the curriculum") to convey a more positive spin on their actions.

WHAT IS CENSORSHIP?

As an exercise in thinking about censorship, read the following scenarios and use them as a basis for discussion, either in a teacher or community group or with students.

- A media specialist's principal has instructed her to remove *Looking for Alaska* (Green, 2005) because of its sexual content. The media specialist does not agree but slides the book under the shelf and tells herself that if a student specifically asks for it, it will be available.
- An English department head has been told by his principal that a parent found Harper Lee's *To Kill a Mockingbird* objectionable because of its use of racially tinged language and ideas. He does not demand that the book be discontinued but requests that it only be used for small-group study rather than whole-class study.
- A summer reading list of 20 books for middle-school students includes the novel *The Hunger Games* (Collins, 2008). A parent feels the novel contains too much violence and threatens to go to the media with offending passages unless it is removed from the list. The principal decides to withdraw the list for summer reading rather than ban the book and tells students instead to choose two books over the summer to read for enjoyment.
- A 5th-grade teacher is using *The Giver* (Lowry, 2011) with her entire class. A parent argues that while she admires the book, it is inappropriate for 5th-graders, who are not developmentally ready to deal with the concepts in the novel. A school committee decides to place the novel in 6th grade instead and the parent is satisfied.
- A teacher wants to place the novel *The Absolutely True Diary of a Part-Time Indian* (Alexie, 2008) in her classroom library, but she feels she cannot defend a few lines that contain strong language. She blacks out the offending lines and places the book on the shelves.
- During independent reading time, a 7th-grade student takes out her own copy of *The Girl with the Dragon Tattoo* (Larsson, 2009). The teacher knows that the student's parents have approved of the choice, but she is concerned that the student will pass the book to other students whose parents may not approve. The teacher asks the student to read the novel at home and choose one from the classroom library shelves instead.

- An English teacher receives a grant for $2,000 to buy books for her classroom library. She goes to the website www.commonsensemedia.org and chooses books based on the website's ratings.

We could have a lively discussion about each of these scenarios and would be hard-pressed to find any group of teachers who would classify all of the scenarios as censorship or even agree on a common definition. What we must do, then, is try to make sense of the underlying principles of censorship. In its most basic form, *censorship* refers to the restriction or suppression of ideas, information, or artistic expression by those in authority, usually a governmental entity. In schools, we often think of censorship as it applies to academic freedom.

ACADEMIC FREEDOM

David Moshman explores academic freedom in his book *Liberty and Learning: Academic Freedom for Teachers and Students* (2009). He explains that "Intellectual freedom is a necessary condition for academic work because education and research require the freedom of students, teachers, and researchers to assess the justifiability of potential beliefs, apply diverse forms of reasoning, seek out what they deem to be relevant information, reach whatever conclusions seem more justifiable and discuss their ideas with others. In the absence of intellectual freedom, genuine education and research are impossible" (p. 46). In his analysis, he presents five principles of academic freedom:

1. *The Freedom of Belief and Identity*—This freedom guarantees the rights of educational institutions to present different views and values but not require that students believe them. Further, students may be assessed on their understanding of what is being taught but not "on the basis of their agreement with particular viewpoints" (p. 48).
2. *Freedom of Expression and Discussion*—Here students (in academic contexts) have a right to express any views relevant to the curriculum, "even if those views are deemed to be false, absurd, offensive, or otherwise objectionable" (p. 48).
3. *Freedom of Inquiry*—"Inquiry must not be suppressed by restricting access to particular authors, topics, or viewpoints, or by hindering the formulation of objectionable conclusions" (p. 59).

4. *Freedom from Indoctrination*—Moshman is adamant about this freedom, explaining that educators may not "require or coerce students to modify their beliefs or values" (p. 51).

5. *Equality, Privacy, and Due Process*—All students have the freedom to express their own views and participate in discussion. Students who hold unpopular views may require special support from educators or the institution. Privacy means that students have the right to choose to "speak, write, and reflect about their own beliefs, values, and viewpoints" (pp. 54–55). Interestingly, intellectual freedom also "includes a right not to discuss what one chooses to keep private" (p. 55). Due process protects students' and faculties' freedoms of belief and expression, especially those that are unpopular.

TYPES OF CENSORSHIP

As we noted above, censorship can come in many different forms and slip unnoticed into the room. When one person or group begins deciding what another person or group can or cannot read, however innocent that may seem, we need to look under the rug for signs of censorship.

Selection

When making selections of books for inclusion in the library or for instructional purposes, those who omit selecting certain books because of ideas, language, or fear of challenges move down the slippery slope of censorship. The National Council of Teachers of English notes in their Guidelines on Censorship that "A bias against certain types of books or their content, authors or illustrators" is, indeed, a form of censorship.

The best way to understand "selection" is that selectors *include* titles for pedagogically sound reasons and generally think in positive terms about books; censors *exclude* titles that may offend and often think of books in negative ways. Figure 2.1 provides an example of this distinction.

In defending her use of Arundhati Roy's *The God of Small Things* and Annie Proulx's short story "Brokeback Mountain," 12th-grade teacher Kimberly Horne explained that Roy's text "brought a taboo topic out of the dark recesses where, culturally, we like to stow these things. Both texts, while difficult, are written in lyrical prose about characters who are overwhelmed and overlooked by the world they live in" (Horne, n.d., p. 40).

Figure 2.1. Censorship vs. Guidelines

Censorship	Guidelines
A teacher excludes books that address suicide or are excessively dark from her classroom library because depressed readers may become convinced to take their own lives.	A teacher includes books that address suicide in her classroom library because students need a broad cross-section of books about a variety of subjects relevant to their lives.
A teacher excludes books for literature circles that portray characters who use drugs or engage in other illegal behaviors because such books demonstrate poor role models. Parents may also question these choices.	A teacher includes books for literature circles that portray characters who use drugs or engage in other illegal behaviors because such books create opportunities for discussion and writing about diverse characters and the conflicts they face. If parents object, she has alternate choices available.
A teacher excludes a book that she thinks might otherwise be effective for a unit on war because the characters use profanity.	A teacher includes a book for her unit on war because the plot and characters are strong and the writing is exemplary. She sees this as an opportunity to show students how to look at parts of a book as they fit into the whole rather than looking only at language in isolation.
A teacher decides not to use a classic novel such as Mark Twain's *The Adventures of Huckleberry Finn* with the entire class because it has been challenged in the past at his school.	A teacher decides to include a classic novel such as Mark Twain's *The Adventures of Huckleberry Finn* for use with his entire class because he feels it best meets his curricular goals.

She goes on to say that the realistic descriptions forced her students to question the author's intentions and believed the books helped her students discern literary merit. Her explanation is a clear example of using guidelines to choose books that best fit the curriculum rather than excluding them because they contain graphic descriptions.

David Moshman, writing about selection, says, "What is central here is genuine respect for your students, whether or not any of them complain. Your interests, values, and personal commitments will inevitably influence your choice of what your students read but you have an obligation to make those choices with the best interests of your students in mind. It may be in your students' best interest to be exposed to issues you deem especially important but it is not in their best interest to be indoctrinated in your specific views" (2009, p. 71).

Self-Censorship

Self-censorship occurs when educators decide not to make a book available to students even though it fits the criteria for inclusion in order to avoid a challenge or because of a personal bias. We find it odd that Julie Anne Peters, for instance, author of 19 books, many of them with gay characters, does not show up on the challenged book lists. Perhaps it is because media specialists and teachers who read reviews of young adult literature know that Peters, an author who does not shy away from lesbian-gay-bisexual-transgender (LGBT) characters and issues, will most certainly incite a challenge, and they choose not to place her books on shelves in an effort to avoid an incident. Removing a book from the shelves is one type of censorship; refusing to place it on the shelves before it even has a chance to be read is perhaps an even more pernicious type of censorship.

A teacher in New Jersey sadly told us that she had discontinued using *Huckleberry Finn* because she had to defend the book 3 years in a row to parents whose "pastor told them to challenge the novel." She reported having to fill out forms, attend formal hearings, and explain to challengers why she felt the novel met her teaching objectives. In the end, she said she knew she was self-censoring the novel but that it just wasn't worth the effort and time it took to keep the book in her classroom.

The Chilling Effect

Challenges often lead to a contagious form of censorship known as the chilling effect, as it runs through schools, districts, and even states. When Robert Cormier's *I Am the Cheese* (2007) was censored in our district, for example, none of his books was taught for years after the ban had been lifted—except by Gloria and ReLeah. When ReLeah began teaching English at the local high school after our censorship battle, her department head told her she was "asking for trouble" by using Cormier's *After the First Death* (1979) with her students, even though the book had never been challenged. Using a book by an author who had created such a controversy was enough to keep everything he had written out of the schools for years.

Teachers are aware of the chilling effect but often bow to its power anyway. When *The Absolutely True Diary of a Part-Time Indian* (Alexie, 2008) was banned from the Stockton (Missouri) High School curriculum as well as from the high school library, communications arts teacher Kim Jasper said, "What can we teach now if this is our bar? Do I need to take *Of Mice and Men* out of my classroom? Do I need to take *Huck Finn* out of my classroom? I just fear the chilling effect of what teachers will choose now" (Stillman, 2010).

This form of censorship can be especially dangerous because teachers, fearful of censorship, try to predict what may be challenged and keep only the safest books on their shelves or retreat to the tried and true classics that have seldom faced a challenge. Students, as always, are the losers in this situation as they are denied the opportunity to read a wide variety of books. The worst part is that they often become turned off to reading when they are provided only with books that stand no chance of ever being questioned.

Book Ratings

You may not have considered that book rating sites can be a form of censorship. If you look at www.commonsensemedia.org or www.theliteratemother.org you will find sites that look deceptively objective. They offer to do the work for parents and teachers by going through books and not only rating them but also objecting to parts of books in isolation. Commonsensemedia, the most popular of these sites, breaks books into parts by using key words that are red flags for readers. The authors of the site come across as experts that parents can trust, implying that they are the ones most competent to make a decision about a student's reading. In addition, many parents go to these sites and object to books chosen by teachers based entirely on the site's recommendation rather than by reading the book to determine whether it is right for their child.

Pat Scales, in her column for *Booklist*, writes,

> While Common Sense Media isn't censoring anything, it is providing a tool for censors. There is already a documented case in the Midwest where a book was removed from a school library based solely on a Common Sense review. Common Sense Media allows users to filter books by "on," "off," and "iffy" [they now use the term "pause"] ratings. And reviewers are instructed to point out anything "controversial." Such warnings encourage site browsers to take things out of context instead of looking at books as a whole. (2010)

Let's look at the award-winning novel *Shine* by Lauren Myracle (2011) as an example. ReLeah recently read this novel and has been recommending it widely. Myracle discusses bullying, friendship, and courage from the perspective of a high school girl whose one-time best friend had been brutally beaten because he is gay. The main character goes through a journey of self-discovery as she reflects on her own attitudes and actions while putting together pieces of the crime in an effort to solve it. It is a book that would engender much discussion in literature circles and is a favorite in classroom libraries.

Now let's look at Commonsensemedia's take on this novel by examining their "rating" system that offers a 1–5 rating on certain aspects of the book, 5 being "the most" in each category.

- Educational value—2 out of 5
- Positive messages—3 out of 5
- Positive role models—2 out of 5
- Violence—3 out of 5
- Sex—1 out of 5
- Language—4 out of 5
- Consumerism—1 out of 5
- Drinking, drugs, smoking—3 out of 5

Commonsensemedia characterizes this novel as a "murder mystery" and recommends it for readers aged 15 and older. The problem with setting a definitive age is that such categories ignore individual maturity, experiences, background knowledge, reading abilities, and interests.

Another novel that ReLeah recently read, *Between Shades of Gray* (Sepetys, 2011), is the story of people in the Baltics under Stalin's regime. ReLeah found this to be one of the most powerful and heart-wrenching novels she has ever read because of the unspeakable terrors visited on Stalin's victims. She recommends this book as well, especially to social studies teachers, and talks about how it affected her emotionally. According to Commonsensemedia, it is "a story of horrific cruelty and violence. Babies, children, the elderly, and even grieving parents die awful deaths, and many more suffer terribly as they struggle to survive."

And how did this book fare when dissected?

- Educational value—5 out of 5
- Positive messages—5 out of 5
- Positive role models—5 out of 5
- Violence—5 out of 5
- Sex—1 out of 5
- Language—2 out of 5
- Consumerism—Not applicable
- Drinking, drugs, smoking—1 out of 5

Commonsensemedia tells parents that the horrors in the book are staggering, but "it's an effective and sensitive way to bring history to life." They recommend the novel to readers aged 12 and older.

The point is not that ReLeah would make one recommendation of these sample books and Commonsensemedia would make another. It is, instead, that sites such as these act as the "Book Police," keeping books out of the hands of readers when they don't even know the readers. Reviews of books are one thing; rating books by dissection without regard to the book as a whole is a sturdy platform for censorship.

CHALLENGES

A challenge is a formal, written complaint, usually on a form provided by the school district, filed against a text used within a classroom or housed within a library. A challenge requests that the materials be removed or restricted, usually because of content, language, or appropriateness. In districts that have a materials review policy, the challenge will go through a process, such as being reviewed by a school committee first, going then to the principal, and finally to the school board or superintendent. A ban is when the challenge is upheld and the text is removed or restricted from the classroom or library.

See Chapter 4 for a detailed explanation of such a process as well as suggestions for creating a solid materials review policy. Often, challenges gain extensive media attention, especially locally, and can stir explosive passions in groups of people who feel their values are being threatened.

What Gets Challenged?

The one certainty about challenges is that you simply cannot predict when they will be issued or why. Who could have guessed, for example, that *The Happy Prince and Other Tales* by Oscar Wilde (2001) would be challenged in Oregon because the stories were "distressing and morbid" or that *James and the Giant Peach* by Roald Dahl (2011) would be challenged many times for reasons that include "promotes the use of drugs and whiskey, contains crude language and encourages children to disobey their parents." Or that Dr. Seuss's *The Lorax* (1971) would be challenged in 1989 in California because it "criminalizes the forestry industry."

Figure 2.2 lists the top ten challenged books in 2010. The American Library Association's Office for Intellectual Freedom keeps track of such challenges and offers all sorts of lists, such as "classics most often challenged" or "most frequently challenged authors." Take a tour at http://www.ala.org/offices/oif.

Figure 2.2. Most Frequently Challenged Books in 2010

Rank	Title of Book	Author	Reason for Challenge
1	*And Tango Makes Three* Published 2005	Peter Parnell and Justin Richardson	Homosexuality, religious viewpoint, unsuited to age group
2	*The Absolutely True Diary of a Part-Time Indian* Published 2008	Sherman Alexie	Offensive language, racism, sex education, sexually explicit, unsuited to age group, violence
3	*Brave New World* Published 1931	Aldous Huxley	Insensitivity, offensive language, racism, sexually explicit
4	*Crank* Published 2010	Ellen Hopkins	Drugs, offensive language, sexually explicit
5	*The Hunger Games* Published 2008	Suzanne Collins	Sexually explicit, unsuited to age group, violence
6	*Lush* Published 2006	Natasha Friend	Drugs, offensive language, sexually explicit, unsuited to age group
7	*What My Mother Doesn't Know* Published 2003	Sonya Sones	Sexism, sexually explicit, unsuited to age group
8	*Nickel and Dimed: On (Not) Getting By in America* Published 2001	Barbara Ehrenreich	Drugs, inaccurate, offensive language, political viewpoint, religious viewpoint
9	*Revolutionary Voices* Published 2000	Amy Sonnie	Homosexuality, sexually explicit
10	*Twilight* Published 2009	Stephenie Meyer	Religious viewpoint, violence

Other books on the most frequently challenged list more than once since 2000 include the following:

- *ttyl; ttfn;* and *18r, g8r* by Lauren Myracle
- *The Perks of Being a Wallflower* by Stephen Chbosky
- *The Catcher in the Rye* by J. D. Salinger
- *The Earth, My Butt, and Other Big Round Things* by Carolyn Mackler
- *The Color Purple* by Alice Walker
- *The Chocolate War* by Robert Cormier
- *Of Mice and Men* by John Steinbeck

- *Fallen Angels* by Walter Dean Myers
- *Arming America: The Origins of a National Gun Culture* by Michael A. Bellesiles
- *King and King* by Linda DeHaan
- *Harry Potter* by J.K. Rowling
- *Bridge to Terabithia* by Katherine Paterson
- *Alice* (series) by Phyllis Reynolds Naylor
- *Go Ask Alice*—Anonymous
- *Scary Stories* (series), by Alvin Schwartz
- *Gossip Girl* (series) by Cecily Von Ziegesar
- *The Adventures of Huckleberry Finn* by Mark Twain
- *I Know Why the Caged Bird Sings* by Maya Angelou
- *Captain Underpants* (series) by Dav Pilkey
- *It's Perfectly Normal: Changing Bodies, Growing Up, Sex, and Sexual Health* by Robie Harris

This discussion may lead you to ask if any book is safe and, unfortunately, our answer is no. That's why teachers could spend their entire careers looking for books that are unchallengeable, and all they would get in the end are empty shelves.

Types of Challenges

In our continuing effort to understand challenges and censorship, let's look at some of the reasons that books are challenged. As you can see in Figure 2.3, material that is sexually explicit tops the list of reasons for challenge from 1990–2010. Next comes "offensive language," followed closely by "unsuited to age group." The problem is, and has always been, that what is "offensive language" to one person is not offensive to another, especially when context is considered. The same is true for "sexually explicit" or "unsuited to age group."

In the Stockton, Missouri, case cited earlier, for example, school board member Ken Spurgeon said, "We can take this book [*The Absolutely True Diary of a Part-Time Indian* (Alexie, 2008)] and we can wrap it in those twenty awards everybody said it won, and you know what, it is still wrong." A handout provided before the meeting cited 74 instances of vulgarity. Compare that response to student Dakota Freeze's comment: "This book in a nutshell is about hope. It's about overcoming adversity. This book is about believing in yourself, believing you can become whatever you want to become" (Stillman, 2010).

Figure 2.3. Challenges by Reason, 1990–2010

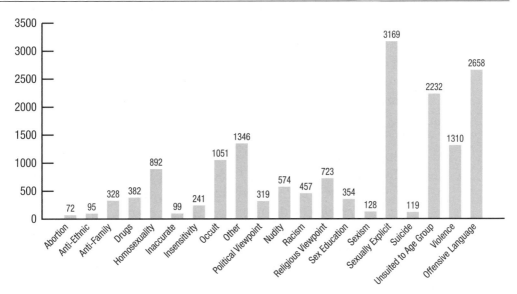

Source: American Library Association, http://www.ala.org/advocacy/banned/frequentlychallenged/challengesbytype

Understanding Challenges

We believe that most challenges are based on fear. For example, if you read the website Parents Against Bad Books in Schools (PABBIS) at http://www.pabbis.com/news.htm, you'll see statements that elicit fear, such as the following:

- You knew violence and pornography were everywhere these days but you didn't know the schools were in the business.
- Some minimum standard of decency has been violated.
- Your trust has been betrayed by the schools.
- You have every right to feel angry and upset. Yes, they are corrupting your child. The schools and elected officials like the school board should not have the power to violate your God-given, natural, and constitutional rights as parents. Unfortunately they do it more and more frequently. And generally they get away with it. More books with graphic sex and violence and other objectionable material are in the schools every day.

- Your children will certainly be impacted if you let them read trash, especially if they accept and consider it a normal part of their "education." The school system forces their values on your child every day.
- Not to be paranoid, but any teachers or schools assigning these books seem to have some kind of agenda. To us, in some cases, no matter what convoluted explanations are given, that agenda seems like corrupting the morals of our child.

While not every parent who challenges a book agrees with these statements, the root of a challenge often comes from the fear that one or more of these things may happen. Parents naturally want to instill their own values in their children and protect them from what they consider to be harmful, but in many cases a witch hunt ensues as fear trumps reason. Fears also abound when parents believe their religious values are being questioned, and such fear turns into paranoia when people begin to believe that someone is intentionally setting out to corrupt their child.

Judy Blume, author of many award-winning and best-selling children's books worldwide, discusses this aspect of censorship.

> I believe that censorship grows out of fear, and because fear is contagious, some parents are easily swayed. Book banning satisfies their need to feel in control of their children's lives. This fear is often disguised as moral outrage. They want to believe that if their children don't read about it, their children won't know about it. And if they don't know about it, it won't happen. (n.d., p. 56)

Laurie Halse Anderson, author of *Speak* (2000) and many other award-winning young-adult books, agrees with Blume:

> Most of the censorship I see is fear driven. I respect that. The world is a very scary place. It is a terrifying place in which to raise children, and in particular, teenagers. It is human nature to nurture and protect children as they grow into adulthood. But censoring books that deal with difficult, adolescent issues does not protect anybody. Quite the opposite. It leaves kids in darkness and makes them vulnerable. (quoted in Nilsen & Donelson, 2009, p. 421)

In Chapter 5 we discuss ways to calmly and sensitively diffuse those fears by honoring parents' wishes for their own children and seeking to understand the root of the fears.

PRINCIPLES OF INTELLECTUAL FREEDOM

Because one standard of appropriateness cannot objectively be created within a society, especially one as diverse as ours, we must adhere to principles that will protect students' rights to read and, at the same time, allow parents the right to their own standards.

For these reasons, we advocate the following principles which we will discuss in greater detail in the following chapters.

1. Parents have a right to determine what their own child may read or not read. They do not have a right to determine what other people's children may read or not read.
2. Teachers should choose books for whole-class reading that meet their educational objectives and goals. They should have a rationale for their selection on file and offer alternate selections for students or parents who object to the whole-class selection.
3. Media specialists should protect the rights of all students to read a wide variety of books across various genres, resist self-censorship, and support teachers who face challenges.
4. Students should be trusted to choose books they want to read and taught that they are responsible for their own selections. When necessary, they should answer to their parents regarding those choices.
5. Advanced-placement and other college-preparatory courses should adhere to the criteria for college courses. As such, they should be exempted from policies regarding challenged materials.

CHAPTER 3

Developing a Philosophy, Engaging the Community

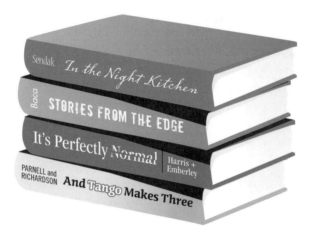

TOO OFTEN, when books and other teaching resources in public schools are challenged or banned, there are no mechanisms in place that require or invite civil public discussion. Nor is there generally much public knowledge of alternatives to censorship that respect the values of individual families. Before we can move into the community, however, we must come to some sort of understanding among ourselves about intellectual freedom. Once a challenge rears its head, it is really too late to develop a coherent philosophy about such a complex issue. These discussions should take place well in advance of a challenge and be revisited often, especially as new faculty come on board.

In this chapter we suggest strategies and provide tools for actively engaging a broad spectrum of the community—including parents, teachers, students, administrators, and other interested citizens—in discussions, simulations, and reflections that will help develop a community-wide commitment to honoring the values of individual families, meeting the needs of diverse learners, and celebrating the joy and power of reading.

DEVELOPING A PHILOSOPHY

School-wide professional learning communities (PLCs) abound on every topic, from reading comprehension to classroom management. Why not a PLC on censorship or intellectual freedom? A teacher group formed to examine this topic could work in interdisciplinary teams or within a single department or grade level. The members may want to engage in a study of this book or read articles from websites such as the National Council of Teachers of English's Anti-censorship center (http://www.ncte.org/action/anti-censorship) and the American Library Association's Office of Intellectual Freedom (http://www.ala.org/offices/oif), or read the Newsletter on Intellectual Freedom from ALA (http://www.ala.org/offices/oif/oifprograms/ifpubs/nif/newsletterintellectual).

The following questions may help guide the discussion:

- What is censorship?

- What is a challenge?

- What is our district's policy regarding challenged materials?

- How would we respond to a challenge?

- What are we willing to risk to ensure that students have rights to read?

- What do we believe about intellectual freedom?

- What does the law say about intellectual freedom?

- How do we honor family standards while still allowing students to read widely?

- What rights does the First Amendment afford teachers? Students?

- Who can we count on to help us with challenges?

After each individual PLC has time to discuss these issues, all groups should come to a whole-staff faculty meeting to exchange views. From there, the principal could lead the group in forming a statement that encapsulates their beliefs about censorship. Nilsen and Donelson advise that such statements should be clear and succinct, devoid of education or literary jargon. These statements may be simple adaptations of our principles of intellectual freedom at the end of Chapter 2, but at the very least examine the topic before an incident emerges.

INVITING THE COMMUNITY TO THE TABLE

The school could also consider inviting the community to participate in the discussion. A format such as a forum moderated by objective chairs, perhaps even high school students trained as facilitators, is the best approach. The National Issues Forum website, www.nifi.org, contains comprehensive information about how to organize and execute a community forum. Figure 3.1 provides questions to help you frame the issues.

Figure 3.1. Questions for Framing an Intellectual Freedom Forum Regarding Reading

1. Who decides what we can read and write in schools?
2. What is the "chilling effect" of censorship? Has it ever occurred in our district or school?
3. What is intellectual freedom? Academic freedom?
4. How do family or community standards play into book selection?
5. Do classroom library books come under the same standards as books selected by a teacher for whole-class instruction?
6. What rules govern selections for a school library? Public library? Classroom library?
7. What are the rights of those who object to a particular book?
8. How does a selection of a book for whole-class reading differ from selection of materials for independent or group reading?
9. At what age should students choose their own reading materials?
10. Does a department head or principal have the right to choose books for students?
11. What rights and responsibilities do teachers have in selecting books for their students?
12. Does your district/school have an approved book list? How does a teacher add books to that list? Who can submit titles?
13. How does a teacher balance respecting the importance of choice and intellectual freedom (for both herself and her students) with keeping her job?
14. Should teachers send letters home to parents before issuing a class novel? What if one parent objects? More than one? A majority?
15. Are there ever justifiable reasons for removing a book from the school library? Class library? Books for whole-class instruction? If so, what are they?
16. What does the law say about censorship? Does the First Amendment protect teachers? Students? Principals? Parents?
17. How can you use the American Library Association's Banned Book Week to raise awareness of censorship issues?
18. What do you believe about taking parts of books out of context?
19. What does it mean that a book has literary quality that overrides objectionable language or descriptions?
20. What plan can we put in place for dealing with challenges rationally and fairly?

STUDENT ACTIVITIES FOR
BANNED BOOKS WEEK

Banned Books Week (an annual event during the last week of September sponsored by the American Library Association) is a great time for introducing students to the issue of censorship as well as engaging the community in lively civic discussion of the value of reading and the importance of protecting individuals' rights to choose.

Writing as a Way of Understanding Censorship

Often Banned Books Week includes such activities as having students read novels that have been banned. Some schools and public libraries sponsor "readouts," where participations read excerpts from books that have been banned to make people aware of the enormous number of excellent books that have been censored throughout the years. While there is a place for such activities, we encourage teachers to create activities that help students deeply understand the complex nature of censorship. Following are some writing suggestions that will provide students opportunities for just such examination.

- Have students respond in writing to censorship scenarios, such as those provided in Chapter 2.
- Have students, perhaps in groups, choose a book that has been banned, read the book, and then write arguments both for and against its use in classrooms.
- Have students look at the reasons books are banned (see Chapter 1) and add reasons they feel books or online text may be banned in the future as their generation comes of age.
- Appendix A contains quotes from famous authors on censorship. Give each student or pair of students a quote and have them write an interpretation, argument, persuasive essay, short story, or poem using the quotes as a prompt.
- Have students engage in a silent discussion by placing students in pairs and providing them with two quotes from Appendix A, one for each student. Each student writes about his or her quote and then they trade papers so the other student can respond.
- Have students look at the websites of their favorite young adult authors to discover what they have to say, if anything, about censorship. Then ask students to imagine they are authors and have them create a section on their "author" website about censorship.

- Have students look at websites of organizations that oppose censorship and create one of their own.
- Have students create a blog about censorship and elicit comments from students around the country.
- Have students create a PowerPoint they could use to defend their favorite book to a school board that is considering a challenge to its use in classrooms.

Classroom Censorship Debate

Students love to engage in debates, especially when they involve controversy. When Gloria first did this censorship activity, she was a visiting teacher invited by the regular teacher to "do something for Banned Books Week," and it has since become a popular way to help students understand censorship. The idea is to provide books that have been censored and have students take roles and either defend or oppose the books for classroom use. You may want to develop a scenario to engage students initially, but then leave it to them to read the books together, research actual challenges to the books in schools, and build their own cases for and against the challenged books.

Introduction. Begin the activity by telling students that an imaginary city called Sunnyday must deal with a formal complaint to the school board about three books used in the local middle school. As news of the challenges spread, other interested citizens join in, and together they form an organization called Citizens for Academic Responsibility (CAR). CAR wants the books to be removed from the Sunnyday Middle School's library, from classroom libraries, and from the curriculum. Another group of teachers and students, calling themselves Free Readers (FR), have joined together to defend the books and keep them in the school.

The challenged books, and the gist of the complaints against each, are as follows:

- *The Adventures of Huckleberry Finn* by Mark Twain—racial epithets and stereotypes
- *The Giver* by Lois Lowry (Newbery Medal winner)—dystopian novel not suitable for children
- *It's Perfectly Normal: Changing Bodies, Growing Up, Sex & Sexual Health* by Robie Harris and Michael Emberley, illustrator—sexual content, including line drawings

[See ALA lists of challenged books for other good titles to use in your own simulation.]

Procedure. Have students do a random draw to determine which book they will be addressing. Students will also draw to determine if they are in favor of censoring the book as members of CAR or of keeping the books in schools as members of FR.

Once students know their book and position, give them a packet about their book which may include a summary/overview of the book or the book itself, reviews of the book, and a copy of the formal challenge to the book. Allow them to have enough time to become familiar with their materials and make a plan for their "public hearing."

The CAR group requesting removal of a particular book will make their presentation first, followed immediately by the defenders of the same book. Either the teacher or another guest, such as a school board member or principal, can interrogate both groups. At the conclusion of all presentations, the entire class acts as the school board and votes to retain or remove each book.

COMMUNITY EVENTS FOR BANNED BOOKS WEEK

Consider having your school host a community event, or ask your local library or college to sponsor one during Banned Books Week. Engaging a broad spectrum of the community in a censorship discussion helps to build a knowledgeable cadre of committed individuals who understand the issues and who often become advocates and allies when an actual challenge arises. The Intellectual Freedom Forum mentioned earlier could be one of several activities slated for this event. Other suggestions follow.

Teachers Discussing Banned Books

Teachers are perfect choices for leading discussions, especially about books they love. Gloria organized a session for a public library event where three local teachers addressed books that had been challenged at various grade levels: Maurice Sendak's *In the Night Kitchen*; two books by Avi, *The Fighting Ground* and *The Seer of Shadows*; and Mark Twain's *Huckleberry Finn*. For *Huck Finn*, Gloria capitalized on the controversy surrounding the announcement by New South Books that they were publishing a new edition of *The Adventures of Huckleberry Finn* with the "n-word" excised.

To provoke thinking and advance discussion in the time allotted, the teachers developed a "front-loading" questionnaire for participants (see Figure 3.2.) This form and others are available for free download at the Teachers College Press website: www.tcpress.com.

The three facilitators then presented an overview of their book(s), elicited comments from those who had read it, and fielded questions from those who hadn't. At the end of the session, participants filled out a Book Ballot (see Figure 3.3), inviting feedback on the books.

An expansion of this activity might include several simultaneous sessions with different categories of books being discussed by teachers or professors, such as the following:

Figure 3.2. Book Selection Questionnaire

Rate each statement below according to this scale.

1 = strongly agree   2 = somewhat agree   3 = no opinion   4 = somewhat disagree   5 = strongly disagree

_____ Children in grades K–12 may be harmed if they are not protected from inappropriate materials.

_____ Even the youngest readers have the right to make choices about what they read.

_____ If a teacher feels that the academic value of a book outweighs the objectionable material contained within it, the teacher should be able to use the book.

_____ When determining which books should be used as part of the school curriculum, educators should respect the values of the communities they serve, even when those values are held by a small minority.

_____ Parents should take an active role in selecting the books their children can and can't read.

_____ Certain books are so objectionable, they should not be protected by the anti-censorship safeguards.

_____ While the use of a novel with a whole class may be the subject of debate, the books in a classroom library would not be, because no student is required to read any particular book.

COMMENTS:

This figure is available as a free printable download on TCPress.com

- Books banned/challenged specifically in elementary, middle, or high school
- Books banned because of racial slurs, violence, or sexual content
- Books banned in a certain state
- Banned classics
- Most frequently challenged books from the last 10 years

Local colleges or universities are often interested in participating in or hosting such "Banned Books" events. Check with the departments of

Figure 3.3. Book Ballot

Please mark your recommendations for each of the books below.

In the Night Kitchen by Maurice Sendak

_____ Appropriate for placement in elementary libraries

_____ Appropriate for placement in K–3 classroom libraries

_____ Not appropriate for elementary libraries

_____ Not appropriate for K–3 classroom libraries

The Fighting Ground by Avi

_____ Appropriate for placement in elementary and middle school libraries

_____ Appropriate for placement in grades 4–8 classroom libraries

_____ Not appropriate for elementary libraries

_____ Not appropriate for grades 4–8 classroom libraries

_____ Appropriate for whole-class reading and study in grades 4–8

The Seer of Shadows by Avi

_____ Appropriate for placement in elementary and middle school libraries

_____ Appropriate for placement in grades 4–8 classroom libraries

_____ Not appropriate for elementary libraries

_____ Not appropriate for grades 4–8 classroom libraries

_____ Appropriate for whole-class reading and study in grades 4–8

The Adventures of Huckleberry Finn (unexpurgated editions) by Mark Twain

_____ Appropriate for placement in middle and high school libraries

_____ Appropriate for placement in grades 6–12 classroom libraries

_____ Appropriate for whole-class study in grades 6–12

_____ Not appropriate for any use in K–12 schools

education, English, and media science, or with their liaison for community events.

If you are interested in creating a community event for Banned Books Week, be sure to check out the great suggestions from the National Council of Teachers of English (www.ncte.org) and the American Library Association (www.ala.org).

CENSORSHIP SIMULATION

Arguably the most powerful way to understand and judge the effects of censorship—without having to undergo the "real-life" experience—is a censorship simulation. Such an activity places students, teachers, parents, administrators, school board members, and other community members in the midst of a controversy over the suitability of a literary work for use in public schools. The prototype for our model was developed by Jean E. Brown (2000), who created it for use in a graduate class, made up of mostly high school and middle school English or social studies teachers. Although we adapted Brown's model liberally, it was a valuable guide as we began to shape our own simulation.

Simulation Logistics

Create a committee made up of a local librarian, college instructor, one or more teachers, a school district representative, a member of the media, one or more students, a politician (such as the mayor or state representative), and other key education or community members. Having two facilitators who share responsibility for organizing the simulation will lighten their load and help keep the event running smoothly.

The very first task is to choose a book for the simulation. Consider featuring a book that would not be an obvious red flag. In general, we're inclined to go with one that's challenged for the ideas it contains rather than one with explicit sexual content or the use of "bad" language. After much deliberation, and considering our community's prior experience with Cormier's *I Am the Cheese*, the committee decided on his novel *Fade* as the focus of our simulation.

Although everyone who plans to come to the simulation could certainly purchase the featured book online or from a bookstore, we wrote a grant to buy copies of the book to give away to those who might be interested in participating. All they had to do was come to the library and pick up a copy. We thought this might encourage people to attend and provide publicity for the event. In addition, it gave participants time to read, reflect, and otherwise prepare for the simulation.

An effective publicity campaign prior to the event itself is a key element in a successful simulation. In our case, the media was more than willing to announce the event in advance, interview organizers, and provide coverage on the date of the event. You can also spread the word through your public library, flyers distributed by teachers and students, school websites, and public service announcements in local media. Figure 3.4 shows the flyer that we distributed for this event.

Figure 3.4. Censorship Simulation Flyer

BANNED BOOKS WEEK

Censorship Simulation

Sunday, September 25
2:00 PM
Bay County Public Library
Meeting Room

Join us as a participant or a spectator in a mock school board meeting where the board hears and considers a parent's complaint about the presence of *Fade*, a young adult novel by Robert Cormier, in the school library and its use in small-group literature discussions in a senior English class.

If you choose to be an active participant, you'll be assigned a role randomly—you might be a supporter of the parent who filed the complaint—or a defender of the book's use. Other roles include the following (and more):
        * school board member
        * high school student
        * school librarian
        * teacher's union representative
        * English department chair

To participate, please register at the Bay County Public Library Reference Desk and pick up your free copy of *Fade* while supplies last. For more information, or to register, contact the Bay County Public Library Reference Desk at 522-2107, or email jpapke@nwrls.com.

Invitations to the event are a nice touch as well and will put the pressure on targeted individuals to attend. Emailed invitations could go to all teachers, or the district may be willing to use their publicity tools to generate interest, especially if they sponsor the event. We decided to create paper invitations and mail them to all school board members, the superintendent, the city council members, and others that we wanted to attend.

Choose a location that will hold enough people and will provide a comfortable setting. Our most recent simulation, an inaugural event of Banned Books Week, was held in the large meeting room at our public library. Seating and microphones were provided for each of the five school board members who were selected by lottery at the opening of the simulation and seated as a panel at the front of the room.

Simulation Participants

Organizers should recruit participants for roles that are likely to require advance preparation; for example, the citizen filing the complaint needs time to read the book thoughtfully and prepare a statement that specifies her or his concerns and objections. We asked a veteran teacher that we knew to be deeply thoughtful and articulate and a staunch champion of intellectual freedom to take this role. We were confident that she would adopt the mantel of a censor and make a reasoned, compelling argument

Sara Dykes, high school freshman, in character as a student who found the book *Fade* objectionable

Photograph by
Robin Shader

for removing the book. We were delighted when her daughter, a high school student who had recently earned first-place honors in her school's history fair for a project on censorship, volunteered to prepare and present her own objections to the book.

In other instances, participants will do a random draw to determine their role once they arrive at the event. Some people may not wish to participate, but in our experience, we have found that there are seldom a lack of volunteers to take roles. Sample roles include the following:

teacher	science teacher
district superintendent	English teacher
school administrator	secondary curriculum director
school board members	high school students
citizen filing complaint	community members supporting
teachers' union	challenged book
representative	community members opposing
English department chair	challenged book
school librarian	

Interestingly, the person who wanted to play the role of the principal who had removed *Fade* from classrooms and libraries after the complaint was filed was Mike Stone, a local attorney who, with his partner Pam

Mike Stone, in character as the principal of the high school, expresses his objections to *Fade*

Photograph by
Robin Shader

The mock school board prepares to vote on whether or not to retain *Fade* in Bay County Schools (left to right, Jack Saunders, Harriett Myers, Henry Dusseault, Tom Wismiller, and Cathy Biddy)

Photograph by
Robin Shader

Sutton, represented both of us in federal court cases involving censorship. This irony added a note of levity to the simulation and intrigued the audience. Such an approach kept the entire event from becoming too serious or even hostile while showing the complexities and pitfalls of censorship.

Another participant might adopt the role of an all-round media person such as a newspaper reporter or newscaster for the local television station. Through these roles the facilitator can create and present editorial viewpoints on the challenged books, share mock letters to the editor—as well as blogs and tweets—that represent a range of views, conduct interviews with participants, and in general invite participants to rationally discuss the issues of censorship.

Censorship Simulation Culmination

After a full and free discussion, involving as many speakers and viewpoints as possible within the allotted time, members of the mock school board will vote publicly on the challenge to the chosen book and explain their reasoning.

Reflections on the Simulation

Follow up with a questionnaire about participants' experiences with the simulation and conclude with a discussion of how viewpoints have changed or been reinforced through this experience. One informal measure of the effectiveness of our simulation centering on Robert Cormier's *Fade* was the buzz that filled the room following the culmination of the event. More than 30 minutes after its conclusion, members of the community were still engrossed in lively conversation.

A Variation of Censorship Simulation

A similar simulation involved over 200 students from a local high school who were bused to the Bay County Public Library for this event. Community members were invited to attend as well. Students read a story by Jimmy Santiago Baca (2010), "The Swing Test," which had been censored in a South Florida high school. Because the story was short, they read it immediately before the simulation. In this case, students were not given roles, but were allowed to create their own role and speak from either side of the issue. Their teachers and administrations got involved as well, exaggerating their claims, which led to much laughter and passionate discussion. The all-student school board voted to retain the story, which was no surprise to anyone in the audience.

COMING TOGETHER

Such examination of challenges and censorship, whether in the classroom with students or with a community event, will not happen without educators, students, librarians, and others who value intellectual freedom. It is vitally important to engage as many people as possible in an honest evaluation of these topics. In all such activities, however, the focus should be on deliberation and finding common ground rather than on winning a debate. With such an approach, there may, indeed, be fewer conflagrations such as the one we endured, and more genuine understanding of the nature of censorship as well as academic and intellectual freedom.

CHAPTER 4

Preparing for a Challenge

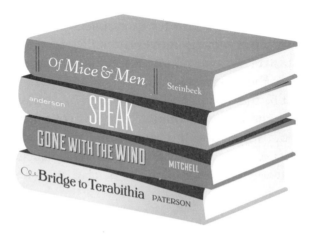

TEACHERS ARE OFTEN blindsided when a challenge arises seemingly out of thin air. One day students are reading *The Adventures of Huckleberry Finn* and engaging in animated discussions about the social mores of the time, and the next day someone is knocking on the principal's door demanding to know why the school is allowing racially charged words to be read in classrooms. As you offer your defense, you may find yourself stumbling over what appears obvious—the book is a classic, the message is actually one of anti-racism, students are discussing important issues that will help them become thoughtful citizens. Your heart races, you struggle to remain objective, but you fall into despair as you come to understand that the person who is lodging the challenge honestly believes that the book has the potential of inciting racial unrest and, further, that *no* student should be subjected to the language Mark Twain used in his famous novel. All too often, at this point the face-off begins.

Of course, there is no guarantee that the issue can be resolved to everyone's satisfaction under any circumstances, but there are preemptive measures that might neutralize the situation and provide an opportunity for meaningful dialogue—or at the very least prevent a freefall to disaster. These actions should be an ongoing and essential part of every school and district's literacy plans.

DISTRICT POLICY ON CHALLENGED MATERIALS

If your district has a policy regarding challenged materials, compare it to the one in Figure 4.1 and make sure you feel comfortable with the protection it provides you and your students. If you are satisfied with it, you should become thoroughly familiar with it and have it available to show to anyone who presents a challenge. If your district does not have a policy or it has one that is unsatisfactory, approach the school board as soon as possible with one or more examples of challenged materials policies (often called an "Instructional Materials Selection and Review Policy") and ask them to revise the existing policy or adopt one as soon as possible. While you may not be in a position to insist that your district write a policy, you can at least suggest that a committee made up of teachers, administrators, parents, media specialists, and middle/high school students address this important issue. You might also approach your teachers' union for help in writing this document. In any case, such a step should be taken *before*

Figure 4.1. Sample Challenged Materials Policy

1. If a parent or other citizen objects to classroom material, he or she should attempt to resolve the issue with the teacher and principal. If the issue is not resolved at this level, the complainant must complete a Reconsideration of Instructional Materials form (see Figure 4.2), citing specific objections.

2. The request is submitted to the school's Instructional Materials Review Committee, made up of teachers, the media specialist, parents, and students. This committee will read the book in its entirety as well as the challenge before beginning discussion.

3. Once the committee forms its recommendation, it is forwarded to the principal, who decides whether the material will be retained or removed.

4. If the principal retains the material, the complainant has 5 days to appeal the decision at the district level. If the principal determines that the material is to be removed, the recommendation is automatically referred to the District Instructional Materials Review Committee, made up of teachers, parents, administrators, district personnel, and high school students.

5. The district committee makes a recommendation to the superintendent. If the superintendent elects to remove the material, the case goes to the school board. If the superintendent elects to retain the material, the complainant may appeal to the school board, which makes the final determination.

Important note: The challenged material remains available for use while the review is under way.

This figure is available as a free printable download on TCPress.com

a challenge arises, not in the heat of a community battle, when objectivity may be in short supply. Not having a challenged materials policy is like playing a hand of cards with no rules—every action is open to anyone's interpretation and the winner is often the one who shouts the loudest.

RECONSIDERATION OF CHALLENGED MATERIALS

A comprehensive form for challenges is also important for both sides. It should not be enough for a parent or other party to simply email or call the principal and demand that a text be removed or restricted. He or she should obtain the form and fill it out in its entirety. While it is impossible to ensure that the complainant has read the complete work in question, for example, the form at least specifies what *should* take place and puts the responsibility for articulating a clear challenge on the part of the person making the challenge. See Figure 4.2 for a sample Reconsideration of Challenged Materials Form.

HONORING FAMILY STANDARDS

Many challenges begin because parents feel that their family values or standards have been violated. What are family standards? How does a school or district uphold them if they conflict with the philosophy your department, school, or district has developed regarding intellectual freedom? While it is important to let the challenger know that her family's values will be upheld, "honoring family standards" does not mean that a family can impose its values on children other than their own. What it does mean is that the school recognizes that each family has its own culture and values that may differ from those of the teacher, other students, or the majority of the school community. Parents have the right to preserve their standards and expect that specific requests regarding what *their* child reads is honored by teachers.

For example, suppose Steinbeck's novel *Of Mice and Men* has been in your school's English 10th-grade curriculum for many years. You decide to use the book with your class, but before students begin reading the first chapter, a parent calls and tells you that her church finds the word "Goddamn" to be sacrilegious and she does not want her child reading *Of Mice and Men* because of the language. Honoring family standards in this case would be a simple matter of offering the student another book

Figure 4.2. Reconsideration of Challenged Materials Form

Title of work: _____ Author: _____

Name of person requesting reconsideration of material: _____

Does the complainant represent a group or organization? If so, please identify.

1. Have you discussed use of the work with the teacher, principal, and/or media specialist?

   If not, please see district policy on challenged material.

   If so, please provide details of the meeting below.

2. Have you read the work in its entirety? If not, please specify which part or parts of the work you have read.

3. Have you read reviews of the work? If so, please attach or provide summaries below, including sources and dates of reviews.

4. How is this work being used in the classroom or library?

5. What is your understanding of why this work is being used?

6. Was your child required to read the work, or did he or she choose to read the work?

7. If the work was required reading, was your child offered an alternate selection? If so, please list titles below.

8. If an alternate selection was offered and you or your child refused the alternate selection, please explain why.

9. Specifically state your objection(s) to the work or to the way in which the work is being used with your child.

10. What actions are you requesting that the teacher, principal, or media specialist take regarding the work?

Signature: _____

Date: _____

Address and
Contact
Information

This figure is available as a free printable download on TCPress.com

from an alternate book list. There should be no questions asked, and the class should know in advance that different students may be reading different books. In a perfect world, parents would feel comfortable with this compromise and thank the teacher for her sensitivity; all would agree that a rich education exposes us to that which might challenge our beliefs. Furthermore, students would be aware of their family's standards and take responsibility for adhering to them (or questioning them), and the teacher would have a wide variety of books available in an effort to ensure that instruction is differentiated. The world is rarely perfect, however, so we must make plans to deal with its imperfections.

LETTERS TO PARENTS

A letter such as the one in Figure 4.3 may help you avoid challenges by reassuring parents that the school values their rights regarding their children's reading selections. This letter would be sent to each student's parents at the beginning of the school year or semester.

While we advocate generic letters to parents such as the one in Figure 4.3, we do not feel that it is necessary to send letters home to parents asking permission for every book that you teach. In fact, such a policy can be

Figure 4.3. Sample Letter: Honoring Family Standards

Dear Parents,

It is the goal of our (school, department) to provide students with every opportunity to experience a wide range of fiction, nonfiction, and poetry, as well as opportunities to experience visual and digital text related to content area studies. Teachers choose certain works for students to read or view because of their literary merit, their contribution to the subject of study, or because they are a part of the district or state curriculum.

We are sensitive to the values of the many different families that make up our school community, and we know that not all texts are right for all students. Thus, we have a policy of alternate selections, meaning that if you, as a parent or guardian, or your child feel that a text is in violation of your family's standards, you have the right to request an alternate work from a list provided by the teacher. Your child will be required to complete assignments comparable to those of other students, and there will be no penalty whatsoever for students who choose alternate selections.

We encourage your participation in your child's education and look forward to working together as all of our students experience the rewards of reading.

Signed by principal, department or grade chair, and individual teacher

This figure is available as a free printable download on TCPress.com

counterproductive. One large district required teachers to send letters to parents listing every book that would be used in each course and parents were to initial those they gave permission for their students to read.

It's not a matter of hiding from parents what's being taught, and a list of instructional materials should always be on hand, but gaining parental permission for each book is a logistical nightmare, an invitation to censorship, and an affront to teachers' professional judgment.

HONORING STUDENT VALUES

One of the goals of education is to help students become independent learners and decision makers. As David Moshman points out, one aspect of academic freedom is not only to allow but also to encourage students to express their views and beliefs freely (2009). All students should have the right to tell their teacher that a work is offensive or troubling to them.

During a discussion of censorship, an adult told us that reading "The Tell-Tale Heart" by Edgar Allen Poe in middle school was so traumatic that it caused him to have nightmares. He said his parents had no idea that Poe's short stories were bothering him and, because they were assigned to the entire class and his classmates seemed to enjoy reading them, he felt that he was being too sensitive. He didn't say anything to anyone. This experience caused him never to read anything by Poe for the rest of this life. Now, as an adult, he wished he had told the teacher and been able to read something different. Situations like this remind us that we have an obligation to reassure our students that they should always speak up if something is offensive to them.

As Jenkins noted in her research, however, one reader's response does not predict another reader's response, which is a significant finding when considering censorship, so we have to teach students to become aware of themselves as readers and tell teachers if they are uncomfortable with a book. When such a culture exists in a classroom, students' introspection may even avert challenges.

As an example of how this can work, consider the story a parent told us recently about her daughter's reading preferences. She said that her daughter, Allyson, had always hated to read anything scary at all; she even dreaded reading *The Witch of Blackbird Pond* when it had been assigned for whole-class reading in her 5th-grade class, despite reassurances from her mother that the book was good. Once she was in high school, Allyson's friends enjoyed Stephen King novels, but Allyson didn't want to read anything by that author. When she was in the 9th grade, *The Hunger Games* was required reading, and the mother asked Allyson if she would like for her to request an alternate selection. Allyson said she wanted to try reading the book, and found that she loved it. It is important to allow students to learn how to choose books and how to decide on books that simply aren't for them.

ALTERNATE SELECTIONS

Just as teachers, departments, or grade levels thoughtfully decide on curricular materials that meet their pedagogical goals, they should determine alternate selections in the same manner.

Make sure that you can't be accused of offering an alternative to the assigned book that is in any way more difficult or less interesting. Choose books that are similar in theme, reading level, and length. Most of all, make sure the alternatives meet the goals of your instruction. It is best to have several choices available but resist having the parent choose the alternative. Remember that as the professional, you have the credentials and right to choose materials that are best suited to your teaching objectives, and the purpose of offering an alternate selection is to honor family standards, not to allow parents to take over your job in choosing instructional materials.

RATIONALES FOR INSTRUCTIONAL MATERIALS

Writing rationales for materials used with whole classes or materials that you assign for small group instruction may be one of the most effective tools for meeting challenges. It is not necessary to write rationales for classroom library selections, although you might keep student interest surveys, media center inventories of popular titles, or reviews in a file to support your classroom library selections.

Rationales show complainants that you take your responsibilities seriously and know exactly what you are doing in assigning a specific text for study. Your department or team can make short work of this task by dividing the rationales to be written among various members. Note that most A.P. and college dual-enrolled courses are exempt from having to provide rationales to parents. These courses are optional and are often governed by curriculum choices that reflect specific syllabi. If parents object to a particular work, they should request that their child be placed in a class that is not governed by college standards.

We suggest that teachers complete an informal rationale form (see Figure 4.4, Reflection Guide for Whole-Class Materials) as well as a formal rationale form (see Figure 4.5, Rationale Guide for Whole-Class Materials, page 56). The purpose of the informal rationale form is to provoke thought about the work and engage teachers in a dialogue that will solidify their reasons for using the text. The form may either be filled out and kept privately or simply used as an outline for professional discussion, perhaps in a professional learning community. The formal document, "Rationale Guide for Whole-Class Materials," is the one that should be available for public scrutiny at any time.

Now for the elephant in the room. Who has time to create such in-depth rationales for each book that you use? Fortunately, NCTE has created hundreds of rationales for a wide variety of books that are often used in English classes. See www.ncte.org/action/anti-censorship/rationales.

Figure 4.4. Reflection Guide for Whole-Class Materials

Text: _____ Author: _____

Group that will read text: _____

1. Why did you select this book for these particular students to read?
2. What do you want students to learn from this reading experience?
3. How will you accommodate the needs of individual readers during a whole-class study of a long work?
4. If other students or teachers have read the book, what have they said about it?
5. What books will be available as alternate choices for students if they or their parents find the content objectionable? How do the alternate choices compare to the assigned text?
6. Is there anything in the book that you feel could elicit a challenge from any segment of your educational community? If so, how will you respond to challenges from the following?
   - Students
   - Parents
   - Other teachers
   - Community members
7. If you plan to use the book for student study groups or literature circles, what criteria did you use for its selection?
8. What do you personally like about the book? Do you have any prior association with the book that is memorable?
9. Does anything in the book make you uncomfortable? If so, how do you plan to deal with that content?

This figure is available as a free printable download on TCPress.com

Figure 4.5. Rationale Guide for Whole-Class Materials

Title: _____ Author: _____

Date Published: _____

Grade and Subject area in which the book will be used: _____

1. What state standard or learning goals will be met by using this book?

2. How will you use the book to further these goals?

3. What reviews, awards, recommendations, or book lists support the use of the book?

(Sources for reviews and awards include *The ALAN Review* [www.alan-ya.org], The Young Adult Library Services Association [www.ala.org/yalsa], The International Reading Association's *Journal of Adolescent & Adult Literacy* [www.ira.org], and National Council of Teachers of English's journals, *English Journal* and *Voices from the Middle* [www.ncte.org].)

4. What previous experience with the book supports your use of it?

5. What activities have you planned to ensure that students have a positive learning experience with this book?

6. What objections to the book do you foresee?

7. How does the educational or literacy merit of the book outweigh possible objections?

8. How do you plan to handle sensitive issues within the work?

9. What alternate selections will you provide for those who find the book objectionable?

This figure is available as a free printable download on TCPress.com

These can be downloaded and used immediately. The following books also offer rationales for commonly taught novels.

- *Censored Books: Critical Viewpoints* (Burress, Karolides, & Kean, 2001; Karolides, 2002)
- *Censored Books II: Critical Viewpoints, 1985–2002* (Karolides, 2002)
- *Rationales for Teaching Young Adult Literature* (Reid, with Neufeld, 1999)

If time is in short supply or you need only a brief rationale for literature-circle books, we suggest you use the following questions, adapted from Kenneth Donelson.

- For what classes (or groups of students) is this book especially appropriate?
- To what particular objectives does the book lend itself?
- In what ways will the book be used to meet those objectives?

- What problems of style, tone, or theme could provide possible grounds for censorship?
- How does the teacher plan to meet these problems?
- Assuming that the objectives are met, how would students be different because they read this book? (Donelson, 1979, p. 166)

STUDENT EVALUATION OF TEXTS

Consider student testimony as a source of support for the work in question. A high school student who read Laurie Halse Anderson's *Speak* wrote in her response log that the book had saved her life. That one line from a student might deter a challenge more than 100 rationales written by teachers. When students turn in essays, projects, or other written pieces that show the power of the work or how it has affected them as learners, ask them if you may place their reports in the book's rationale folder. A collection of positive comments from students will significantly strengthen your claim that the text is worthy of study. Figure 4.6 shows a sample student response form. Consider asking students to fill out such an evaluation for

Figure 4.6. Student Response Form

Title of Book: _____

Date: _____ Class: _____

1. What did you learn from reading this book?
2. Do you believe this book should be required reading for students in the future? Why or why not?
3. Compare this book to others you have read. How would you rate it in each of the following categories?
   - Difficulty
   - Interest
   - Ability to make you think
4. Would you read another book by this author or on this topic? Explain.
5. What part of the book did you like best? Least?
6. What activity related to the book was most beneficial to you as a learner?
7. Was there anything about the book that you found objectionable?
8. Other comments:

each book you assign. The data gleaned from these evaluations will help you plan for future classes and confirm the book's pedagogical value.

MAKE NO ASSUMPTIONS

As we have pointed out repeatedly, it is virtually impossible to know which book will elicit a challenge for what reason and by whom. You have only to look at the list of challenged and banned books to be convinced of that fact. As a reminder, *Gone with the Wind, Little House on the Prairie,* and *Twelfth Night* have all been soundly censored. No matter how well prepared you are, there are no guarantees that a challenge won't be lurking nearby. As you prepare for what *could* but may never happen, make no assumption that your hard work will deter a challenge. At the same time, know with certainty that you may be the one person who is safeguarding education and all that it entails: the rights of students to read and think about as well as question all manner of ideas. It is only through such freedom that real education exists.

CHAPTER 5

Facing a Challenge

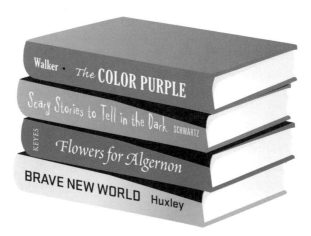

DESPITE YOUR BEST efforts to engage your department, administration, faculty, parents, and community in open, constructive dialogue about your instructional philosophy, methods, and materials, you may still face criticism and complaints, which sometimes escalate into a formal challenge. In some cases, you'll be aware of your critics' fears and objections—and be able to create opportunities to address them respectfully and calmly. Many times we've found that face-to-face conversations with concerned parents allay their fears, especially when we spend as much time listening and honoring others' perspectives as we do aggressively defending our own.

Once, when a group of Gloria's 8th graders were reading Daniel Keyes's novel *Flowers for Algernon*, she encouraged her students to share the book with their parents. After one student told her that his father was concerned about the sexual content, Gloria wrote to the father, explaining her reasons for choosing the book, expressing hope that he would allow his son to read it with the class but also assuring him that she'd be happy to suggest an alternate selection.

The next day Gloria received a note from the father, who read the book after his son went to sleep, and wrote "I agree with your assessment of the book." He also went on to pose some terrific questions: *How much life experience does a person need to have to be able to appreciate and learn from this type of book? Do middle school students have a sufficient amount of experience?* A phone conversation followed, and the parent agreed to allow Gloria to include his questions on the essay test students took after they had read and discussed the book, and give them the opportunity to share their perspectives with an eager audience.

When Gloria sent him the students' mini-essays in response to his queries, the father read and responded personally and thoughtfully to each student, and a potential challenge turned into a positive learning experience—and a model of civil discourse—for all involved.

ADDRESSING CONCERNS ABOUT WHOLE-CLASS READING

But what if your careful professional planning, attention to all school district requirements for selecting instructional materials, and willingness to work with parents who express concerns in selecting mutually agreeable alternatives aren't enough, and you're faced with a parent or administrator who finds no value in a book or activity you've assigned and feels morally obligated to seek its removal from the classroom? If you've taken our advice in Chapter 3 to heart and used a variety of means to help your colleagues as well as community members in general to explore, understand, and value intellectual freedom in schools, you'll have a cadre of informed and committed citizens to call upon. The recommendations we've made in Chapter 4—to participate in developing a strong, clear district policy on the selection and review of instructional materials, as well as building a classroom culture that honors family standards and student responsibility—will put you in the best possible position to respond to the challenge with calm professionalism.

First Steps

If no formal challenge has been filed, arrange a meeting with the concerned parent, and include your team leader, department head, or subject area supervisor. Not only does having a knowledgeable third party present send the message that you're taking the parent's concerns seriously, but it also provides a witness who can attest to your professionalism in dealing with the complaint. Although a formal agenda isn't necessary, having a plan for the meeting will give you confidence and help you remain calm and collected. Asking for permission to record the meeting may elevate tensions, so we suggest taking notes that you can review and expand after the meeting.

Suggested Plan for Initial Meeting with Concerned Parent

1. *Informal introductions.* Use this opportunity to establish connections and build bridges wherever you can. Have you taught other children in the family, attended school or church with the parent, or coached a cousin or aunt?
2. *Brief statement of reason for meeting.* If a note or phone call has prepared you to do this, encapsulate your understanding of the parent's concerns, and then invite him or her to elaborate.
3. *Parent's statement of concerns.* Listen attentively, without interruption, until the parent has time to express herself or himself. Take notes as you listen.
4. *Written rationale, professional reviews, and student responses.* Give a brief overview of why you chose the material and how you use it. Present a copy of the rationale, unit plans, professional reviews, and student responses or evaluations.
5. *Explanation of alternative selection policy.* If the rationale for the material includes alternative selections, bring copies and offer to lend them to the parent. Let the parents know that you're also willing to consider other alternatives they might suggest if they meet the objectives of your class study. This is also a good time to emphasize that students who read an alternate selection aren't singled out or subjected to embarrassment.
6. *Wrap-up.* Thank the parent for the opportunity to explain your curriculum. If the issues haven't been resolved, set a time for a follow-up meeting to discuss the alternative selections and procedures for facilitating a teacher-supported independent study. If you haven't already informed your school administration of a potential challenge, now's the time.

The chances are excellent that concerned parents will respond positively to your careful attention to their issues, respect for their perspective, and willingness to work out mutually agreeable alternatives. If that fails to happen, however, for whatever reason, and a family chooses to file a formal complaint (often called a Request for Reconsideration of Instructional Materials), there are many positive steps you can take in preparing to defend the book publicly.

ORGANIZING FOR ACTION

Begin with your own department, team, or grade group. If the selection being challenged is common reading or viewing, your colleagues also have a significant stake in the outcome and should be informed as soon as possible. Some teachers will join the defense team immediately and enthusiastically, while others will shy away from controversy and in a few cases even support the complainants. It is common for fellow teachers to feel (and often express) that educators who get involved in a censorship controversy are "troublemakers." Others may fear that antagonizing those in charge will lead to a punishment or even dismissal, so they will refuse to offer support (Nilsen & Donelson, 2009). Try not to take any of these occurrences personally. Although it's natural to view lack of support as betrayal, we strongly recommend that you accord the same right to your colleagues as you would to parents—namely, the right to disagree on important issues.

Devote a department, team, or grade-group meeting to reviewing your district's Instructional Materials Selection and Review policy. Make copies available to all members and lead them through the steps of the process, composition of the review team, time line, and other key provisions of the policy. Most policies adopt an "innocent unless proven guilty" stance and allow challenged materials to remain in use while the review process is under way, but make sure that's the case in your district. Another important task in this first meeting with colleagues is to solicit and begin gathering student work samples from the unit of study—reading journals, projects, students' evaluations, and so on that help to establish the value of the work and its role in your curriculum.

Building Your Core Team

To paraphrase Margaret Mead, "Never doubt that a small group of thoughtful, committed teachers can save a book." In that spirit, invite your colleagues to join you in a group that will gather materials, prepare a professional response to the Request for Reconsideration, and recruit and organize supporters if necessary. If meeting at school at the end of the day is your only option, you will undoubtedly make that work, but if your core team is willing, we recommend meeting at someone's home or office on the weekend, where you can enjoy privacy, fewer interruptions, and beverages of your choice.

Responding to the Request for Reconsideration

Your district's review policy may or may not allow for public input and participation at meetings of the review committee. In our state (Florida) open access laws are generally favorable to citizen involvement, but even if you can't attend the meetings, you can submit materials to the members. In addition to the written rationale for including the book in your curriculum, which we hope you already have on hand, you'll want to include your response to the specific criticisms of the book made in the Request for Reconsideration, so you'll also need copies of the complaint—as well as the book—on hand for this initial meeting.

Do your best rhetorical analysis of the Request for Reconsideration and identify the specific complaints about the material. These may not be separate and distinct, but try to capture the gist of each issue in the complainant's own words. In drafting a response or rebuttal, you might assign each criticism to a different volunteer, or one person who knows the challenged material well can do the entire draft. However the draft is generated, it should be vetted, reviewed, revised, and edited with great care.

In the packet to be distributed to all members of the review committee, also include published reviews, which we suggested in Chapter 4 that you collect for every long work your students study. When a work is challenged, widen your review net. In addition to your own favorite professional sources of book reviews, such as *School Library Journal*, *Hornbook*, *The ALAN Review*, ALA's *Book Links*, and *English Journal*, check your public library for *Book Review Index*, a comprehensive source that indexes reviews from 1965 to the present, now available online by subscription. And don't forget America's best bargain—interlibrary loan—as you collect the reviews themselves. If your library doesn't have a review source available, in many cases you can make a free request online that goes out to libraries all over the country. Best of all, the service is free in most libraries. Of course the Internet can be invaluable as you search for reviews by students, teachers, librarians, and professional organizations. Your school or community librarian may be willing to assist you in your search.

Components of Packet Distributed to Review Committee

- Teacher's rationale for use of the material under review
- Your department or team's detailed response to the Request for Reconsideration
- Published reviews of the challenged material
- Student evaluations of the material, if available

House the material in folders or binders and deliver copies to your district office, for distribution to review committee members, the superintendent, and school board members. Make sure your principal and all members of your department receive a copy, and prepare extras for the media. You may want to send electronic copies of the materials, but make sure that everyone has received your email.

KNOWING THY CRITICS

Although many challenges to instructional materials are brought by individuals, existing or ad hoc groups also initiate complaints. In our community, when two novels—and the very existence of classroom libraries—were challenged, a group calling itself at various times Citizens for a Clean Community and Citizens Association for Responsible Ethics ran a large ad in a local shopper proclaiming "THE ISSUE IS NOT CENSORSHIP, BUT ACCOUNTABILITY" and attacking teachers "who stray from the norm and introduce questionable and inappropriate materials." The spokesman of the group also purchased a half-page ad in the local newspaper entitled "Your Child's Textbooks—Have You Read Them?", in which he showcased what Gloria called "disemvoweled" excerpts, such as "Life is sh_t," from Robert Cormier's *The Chocolate War*, a book available in many of our class libraries, and a few excerpts from the two challenged books (Collins, 1986, p. 5).

In the interest of finding common ground and resolving differences without prolonged, destructive struggles, we have a responsibility to consider the views of our critics, and most organizations of concerned citizens are not as vitriolic as those we faced. In the late 1990s, a group in Richland, Washington, calling itself Citizens for Academic Responsibility formed to review 80 novels on a newly adopted secondary reading list and filed formal challenges to seven of them—without attacking teachers or the school system.

The policies in many school districts recognize and honor parents' rights to choose alternate selections for their own children and to work with teachers in determining the procedures for independent study. Although we occasionally hear objections to alternate selections from parents who fear their children may be teased or ostracized, respect for the right to choose is a given for children in schools with a robust reading culture.

CONNECTING WITH ALLIES, WITHIN AND BEYOND YOUR COMMUNITY

Whenever instructional materials are challenged, particularly if a community group files a reconsideration request against more than one book, teachers often feel (and sometimes *are*) under personal attack, as the ads from our local papers cited above suggest. To counter the sense of siege and isolation, we advise reaching out to your natural allies for support.

Few groups anywhere are more zealous in defense of the right to read for learners of all ages than librarians. In our protracted local saga, the director of the public library system was one of our staunchest advocates, attending public meetings, speaking on our behalf, writing letters to the editor on the value of young adult literature, and participating in a series of public forums organized to encourage parents to read YA literature with their children. A youth librarian also served as secretary of the community organization that formed to defend our department and our books, and the director of a branch library offered free meeting space. We consider these types of actions to be part of the job of the school and community librarians and would hope that they would bring the substantial support of the American Library Association to the table.

One of our first local actions after two of our books were challenged was to call, with the support of our principal, a public meeting of our school community, which drew hundreds of parents who packed our school cafeteria on an evening in May. After brief statements from the teachers who were using the two challenged books, we used the remainder of the evening to listen to parents, who drew numbers to determine the order of speaking and were given 3 minutes each to state their views. The overwhelming support buoyed us and left us more determined than ever to protect our books. (For more information on our local struggles, see our 2002 book *At the Schoolhouse Gate: Lessons in Intellectual Freedom*.)

In addition to providing moral support, people in your community can provide tangible help in the form of photocopying, assembling materials, speaking at public hearings, writing letters to the editor, establishing a blog or website, and so on. Other individuals and groups in your community to contact—if they don't reach you first—when a book challenge escalates into a broad attack on your program or department include the following:

- Teachers union
- Booksellers
- Local chapters of civil liberties groups, such as the ACLU
- College and university professors
- Writers' groups

At the national level, a number of organizations stand ready to join the defense whenever books and instructional materials are challenged. See Appendix D (pp. 90–91) for key national organizations that will offer support and resources for challenges and censorship.

RELYING ON EACH OTHER

Despite all of the support, those in the center of a censorship controversy will need an extra dose of encouragement and care from both friends and family. The process of defending a book can be exhausting, often discouraging, and almost always emotionally charged. Don't shy away from asking for the help you need at this time and, above all, try to remember the importance of the task that has somehow fallen in your lap. Your students, your own children (if you have them), and history will record your defense of reading as heroic—with good reason.

CHAPTER 6

Collecting Wisdom

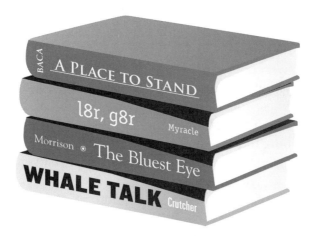

Be it grand or slender, burrowing, blasting, or refusing to sanctify; whether it laughs out loud or is a cry without an alphabet, the choice word or the chosen silence, unmolested language surges toward knowledge, not its destruction. But who does not know of literature banned because it is interrogative; discredited because it is critical; erased because alternative? And how many are outraged by the thought of a self-ravaged tongue? Word-work is sublime because it is generative; it makes meaning that secures our differences, our human difference—the way in which we are like no other life. We die. That may be the meaning of life. But we do language. That may be the measure of our lives.

—Excerpt from Toni Morrison's Nobel Lecture, 1993

WHEN IT COMES to censorship or challenges, it is nearly impossible to get too much advice, especially from those who have been there. We've asked experts in the field and some of our favorite young adult and children's authors to round out our discussion by answering a question specific to their work and experience.

VOICES OF YOUNG ADULT AND CHILDREN AUTHORS

Judy Blume, award-winning author of nearly 28 books translated into 30 languages, wrote books that defined many of our childhoods, including *Are You There, God? It's Me, Margaret; Blubber;* and *Forever.* She has been a long-time advocate of intellectual freedom and has worked tirelessly with the National Coalition Against Censorship in bringing awareness of this issue to the forefront and preventing censorship in schools. Her book on censorship, *Places I Never Meant to Be, Original Stories by Censored Authors,* is one of our favorites.

> *Question:* Many young people grew up with your books on their bedside tables. Your name has drawn accolades and honors for many years but, even so, your books are still being challenged and censored. Perhaps more than anyone we know, you have remained passionate against censorship. Why is this issue so important to you?

> *Answer:* I think it has to do with passion, passion for reading as a young person, when I was free to read any book on the shelf in our house. That silent message from my parents that reading was a good thing. And it has to do with new writers who have to be free to tell the best stories they can without fear. I tell them when they go into that little room where they will be alone with their characters they have to leave their fears at the door. No censors allowed. No critics allowed. I don't even allow an audience in. I may have been an anxious child, may be a worrier even now, but alone with my characters I am fearless. I like to think this is the real me.

*   *   *

Chris Crutcher is an award-winning author of 12 books for adolescents, including *The Sledding Hill*, a novel that looks at censorship from the point of view of a young boy. Many of his books have been censored or challenged. Crutcher is a frequent speaker on issues of censorship and a popular author at conferences as well as in classrooms and schools. Find out more about his take on censorship and all of his books at www.chriscrutcher.com.

> *Question:* On your website you write, "Most banned books are removed from shelves in silence. The public—and the book authors—never even know it's happened." Why is this form of censorship so egregious?

Answer: That form of censorship is egregious because it's cowardly. No one ever gets a chance to hold a discussion about the merits or deficiencies of the book in question and it allows censors to do their work in secret. It also allows people who should know better to be censors. A librarian or teacher or even an administrator can take a book out with no fanfare; thereby removing the material without anyone who might benefit from knowing it's there. Like I said, it's cowardly. Many times the people who choose to censor this way don't call it censorship. I get it that a process of "selection" has to happen, particularly in public schools. But when a philosophical agenda is attached, rather than simply grade-level appropriateness re: language and "understandability," it is censorship.

Jimmy Santiago Baca is author of more than 12 books of poetry, three novels, and a book of short stories for adolescents, *Stories from the Edge* (2010). He won the Pushcart Award, the American Book Award, and for his memoir, *A Place to Stand*, the prestigious International Award. You can find out more about his books and his life at www.jimmysantiagobaca. com/biography.html/.

Question: You had six books banned in Arizona schools during the purge of Mexican studies courses. Why is it so important for all students to be able to access literature from their own cultures?

Answer: It's important for students to have access to their literature because it's a definitive ingredient in shaping who they are in this world. Their cultural literature is as endemic to them as grasses are to the plains, cedar and piñon to the mountainous regions I come from, and these cultural attributes not only find themselves in stories and songs and poems and dances of our people in the Southwest, they also imbue the spirit and heart with their presence when kids read stories. Cultural literature offers a robust look into one's history, it hints at historical events in ways that detail one's days with one's cultural tapestry—the songs heard, the chili eaten, the carvings carved. It emboldens one's spirit with awe for one's personhood and so much more.

In short, one's cultural literature is the necessary elixir that gives one the aptitude of happiness; it's what prevails over our days with a certain spice for life, making us happy to be alive.

* * *

Julie Anne Peters is author of more than a dozen books for young adults and children. Her book *Luna* was a National Book Award finalist, and many of her other books have won awards as well. Her books have been published in more than seven countries and in several languages. You can find out more about Peters and her books at www.julieannepeters.com.

> **Question:** Amazingly, your books do not often appear on banned books lists. We have our own suspicions that your books are not making it to the school library shelves because of their well-known LGBT themes. Why is it important that students have access to your books?

> **Answer:** I'm going to answer your question with two excerpts from letters I've received from young readers:

> > "It's beyond great that there's now young adult fiction about positive gay characters. More than anything, I wish I'd found something like this in my school library in that place in time where I was so confused that I wanted to die. I have moved on from that place, but I am so glad that someone has written a book accessible to teens right at the age where questioning starts."

> > "Your book *Keeping You a Secret* was such a good book. It kind of shows what really goes on in the schools if people are gay and how hard it can be. To me, I feel this book could help gay people feel that it is okay to be gay, and it can also help people who aren't become more understanding and accepting."

* * *

Lauren Myracle is a best-selling author of many books for adolescents, including the popular "IM" books, *ttyl*, *ttfn*, and *l8r, g8r*. She has the dubious distinction of being one of the most challenged authors in the 21st century. You can find her at www.laurenmyracle.com.

> **Question:** While your novel *Shine* speaks directly to the issue of bullying, we know that many teachers will shy away from its use in the classroom because of the straightforward way you deal with homophobia. In fact, many of your novels have the distinction of being on the "banned book" list. What would you say to teachers and librarians to help them understand that your novels are worth the fight?

Answer: I was on a panel about censorship with the inimitable (and awfully handsome) David Levithan recently, and I spoke first, which was fortunate for me as David is such a kick-ass speaker that one would have to be a fool to voluntarily go after him. I told a story about an author visit I'd done at a junior high school, and how, when I arrived, the librarian pulled me aside and said in a low, polite voice, "We are so glad to have you here! Now, so you know, we don't have your *ttyl* titles in our collection, or *Rhymes with Witches*, or *Bliss*, and certainly not *Shine*, because those books have, well . . . content. You know what I mean. That's not going to be a problem for you, is it? Oops, look at the time! Your first presentation starts now—have fun!"

In the censorship panel, after I relayed this story, I was my typical, self-effacing, nonconfrontational self, and I told the audience something along the lines of, "Did it depress me? Yeah. Did it make me feel sucker-punched? Heck, yeah. And do I think that librarian was serving her students in the best possible way she could? No, I don't, because 'content' isn't bad, necessarily."

To paraphrase Katherine Paterson, a book written to offend no one will most likely fail to make a difference to anyone. But do I understand how scary it must be, sometimes, to be a librarian, and to know that if you include a wide variety of books in your collection, you're likely, at some point, to have to go to bat for your beliefs? Yeah, sure. So while I wasn't impressed by how that librarian handled the situation, I didn't condemn her. I just felt bad for her. She just wanted to keep her job, that's all I could figure."

I wrapped up my part of the panel presentation, and then it was David's turn. And David? David leaped up and said, "Okay, before I even begin, I have to address the story Lauren told, because we authors have all had that happen to us. But I am not as nice as Lauren." (Side note: He is. He totally is. And super handsome; did I mention that? Right, back to David's speech . . .) "Lauren forgave that librarian, saying, 'She just wanted to keep her job.' But she wasn't doing her job, and if she wasn't doing her job, she doesn't deserve to keep it."

And everyone burst into applause, hooting and stomping, and I felt foolish and dumb, but not really, because David is the sort of dude who can say something like that and make everyone feel empowered, not just the silly author who forgave the librarian she spoke of too easily, but even the members of the audience who very well might have acted similarly themselves, either by looking the other way or— yes—by choosing not to make certain books available because those particular books made them uncomfortable.

So suffice it to say, I'm now with David on this one. A school library collection can't consist purely of books the librarian is comfortable with, or books the librarian sees as safe. A school library should serve every student, not just the supposedly mainstream students who are happy to read books without "content." (Do such students even exist, really?) A school library should be dangerous, and proudly so. And to the librarians and teachers of our schools—and to myself, because I need the reminder—I would say: Be the freedom fighters you know yourselves secretly to be. Yes, taking a stand can be hard, and scary, and yet it is excruciatingly necessary, if what's at stake is moving into alignment with what you know in your heart.

*   *   *

Lisa Ludeke, editor and publisher of professional books for teachers, recently published her first young adult novel, *Smashed.*

Question: Your young adult novel, *Smashed,* has been very well received by teachers and kids as well as by reviewers. You have said, however, that you believe your book will be censored. All authors want their works to be read, yet censorship creates a chilling effect for teachers and media specialists who might otherwise bring your book into schools. Does the specter of censorship in any way affect your writing as you move forward as a new voice in YA literature?

Answer: First, I want to say that if my book actually does get censored, it means it's being read enough to get on the radar of somebody, somewhere. And knowing my book was being read enough to get noticed would be cause for celebration. Books that are censored are making an impact out there: What writer doesn't want that?

I knew from the time I conceived the idea for *Smashed* that it would be a candidate for censorship because of the violence and underage drinking. And at times I asked myself, *Why am I writing this? Is this necessary?* I'd also worry that no one would be sympathetic to my main character, Katie, who seems to make the same bad choices repeatedly.

But early on, I remember hearing director John Singleton talking on the radio about his first film, *Boyz n the Hood.* He said, "My job is to tell the truth. The truth isn't always a role model." *That's it,* I thought. *That's how I feel.* I pulled my car over and scribbled his words down on a scrap of paper. From then on, whenever I felt unsure, I repeated those words in my head. *My job is to tell the truth. . . .*

So, to circle back to your question, *Does the specter of censorship in any way affect your writing*, the answer is yes, I think about it, but it doesn't ultimately affect my story—the details or what I leave in or out. I'm true to the scene, to the characters, and to life as I know it. If I started circling around the truth, dodging the dark stuff, pretending that wasn't part of it, my readers wouldn't trust me anymore. Especially the kids. They know when someone's trying to bullshit them, and they'd just throw the book down. And I'd lose interest in my own story. I like writing complex stories, stories with more than one layer. Complex stories call for complex characters, and complex characters aren't one-dimensional. They certainly aren't perfect.

My work is fiction, but its power, if it's to have any, lies in its bigger truth. It's a reflection of life—essential truths about life. This isn't true just in realistic fiction, but in other genres as well. It has to get at something about the human condition.

VOICES OF THOSE WHO KNOW
A FEW THINGS ABOUT CENSORSHIP

Joan Bertin, executive director of the National Coalition Against Censorship (NCAC), is also an attorney who practiced law for many years. NCAC offers direct assistance and counseling to anyone confronted with censorship. The coalition unites over 50 organizations dedicated to promoting free expression. Sign up at www.ncac.org to subscribe to their newsletter.

Question: Your role as director of the National Coalition Against Censorship has kept books in the hands of students all across the country. Recently, you have become concerned about the rating of books, which some parents and teachers say helps them decide on "appropriate" choices for their children. What do you say to those who rely on websites such as www.commonsensemedia.org or www. bookbuzz.org to guide their decisions in choosing books?

Answer: In my view, rating books, the way movies and video games are rated, is fundamentally misguided. By their very nature, ratings oversimplify things. They reduce a book to a few letters, numbers, or symbols, which cannot capture context, subtlety, and nuance. One rating site, CommonSenseMedia.org, uses "emoticons" (martini glasses for alcohol, bombs for violence, lips for sex, etc.), but these tell you nothing about the context in which that content appears, the literary value of a book, its appeal, or the intellectual and emotional significance it may have for readers.

Ratings are also culturally loaded and inherently biased. They are expressly intended to "warn" consumers about content that some people find objectionable—sex, violence, profanity, drug and alcohol use, consumerism, "bad" role models, et cetera. Of course, not everyone, or even most people, agree that such content is problematic, but ratings impose a subjective value judgment that warns people away from such content. Sometimes that content is a minor element of a book, but once it's flagged, the book is tainted.

Even worse, ratings say little about the positive value of reading— almost any book. Books expose readers to different experiences, people, communities, and cultures; they take readers to far-off places they may never go in person; they allow readers to experience life through the eyes of another; they provide insights into human behavior; they show the challenges life can present; and they may help readers resolve conflicts and dilemmas in their own lives. All this is lost when a book is reduced to a PG-type rating. Sometimes sex or violence is part of the story, but that is no reason to condemn it. These themes have been part of literature forever, because they are part of life. Just check out the Bible. Or Shakespeare. Or Sophocles.

Individuals can ignore these kinds of ratings, but they do real damage when parents rely on them to challenge books in public schools and libraries. The education of all students suffers when the subjective judgments of self-appointed arbiters of literature, rather than professional educators, determine what gets taught in public schools.

* * *

Millie Davis is the senior developer of Affiliated Groups and Public Outreach director for the National Council of Teachers of English (NCTE). In short, she is the go-to person for reporting censorship incidents and will offer valuable assistance and support on behalf of NCTE.

Question: Many English teachers have utilized NCTE's anti-censorship resources (www.ncte.org/action/anti-censorship) when faced with challenges to books in their classrooms, libraries, or schools. They also may have talked to you as they sought help. We know that you have written many letters to districts and school boards arguing passionately in favor of students' rights to read. What do you feel is most important to convey when persuading would-be censors to reconsider?

Answer: It's odd, but in many ways those of us who fight against censorship and those who fight to censor texts are all fighting for the good of our children and their education. How we want to attain that good is where we come out on different sides. NCTE believes that the best education is based on students' right to read widely, think, study, and discuss even difficult and unpleasant things, while those who challenge texts want to restrict students and "protect" them from any word, event, or thought outside of the would-be censor's belief system. In my experience these would-be censors rarely change their minds, so most of the letters I write are to those who make decisions about texts that "would-be" censors have challenged. I write to reconsideration committees and school boards and, once in a while, to the press. While I have little hope of convincing challengers to change their views—although this has happened on rare occasions—I have every hope of convincing those who make decisions through policy and due process that the beliefs of one challenger or even a handful are not grounds for book removal or curricular change.

I base my arguments on NCTE's belief in the students' right to read and in the care and professional judgment teachers put into choosing, and using, materials appropriate for students to meet the educational objectives of the course, curriculum, and state standards. Context is everything when talking about the value of a text because *the whole of the text* determines literary and educational value, not one scene or the language or situations in one part of the text. Teaching a text in which the characters are portrayed realistically doesn't in any way mean that the actions of those characters are recommended as behaviors students should adopt or be condoned by the teacher, the author of the text, or the school.

While it's important for parents to guide their children's learning, it is not their job to impose their values, morals, or beliefs on other families. Besides, rejecting a text because some object to, or disapprove of, its content violates basic constitutional principles that insist schools not remove texts simply because they dislike the ideas contained in those texts. The educational objective for all in America is to create a democratic citizenry by preparing students to think critically, act responsibly, and be productive in our diverse and ever-changing world. As teachers, we can't reach this objective without exposing students to the broad spectrum of ideas and then guiding them as they read, write, and talk about these ideas.

We need to give more credit to students. They can distinguish between the real world and fiction. Through reading, students can encounter human experiences vicariously, giving them the chance to think about these issues without ever having to actually experience them or, in some cases, in preparation for experiencing them. Literature that grabs us by the gut is literature worth teaching not only because it opens readers' minds and hearts to the human experience but also because it provides the best opportunities for students to think deeply and critically about the text and their world.

*   *   *

Joan Kaywell is professor of English Education at the University of South Florida. She is well known for her love of young adult literature and has been active in NCTE's Assembly on Literature for Adolescents (NCTE) for many years. She is also the author of *Dear Author: Letters of Hope*, an edited collection where young adult authors respond to kids who have written to them about how their books affected their lives.

> **Question:** In your book *Dear Author: Letters of Hope—Top Young Adult Authors Respond to Kids' Toughest Issues*, you provide letters from teens attesting to the power of young adult literature to change and, in some cases, save lives. Nevertheless, many of the authors named by these kids have been challenged or censored. How do you make sense of this paradox?

> **Answer:** The saying, "Thou dost protest too much" comes to mind. Parents who are alcoholics or who abuse their kids certainly don't want their children informed that they must report their abuse to a trusted adult. That's not to say that all censors are abusive parents or alcoholics.
>
> There is another group who'd like to protect their children from the "unpleasantries" of life. The sad truth is that approximately a fourth of girls and a sixth of boys will be sexually violated in some way. The statistics for children affected by alcoholism in some way is even greater. I can say with a great deal of confidence that even the most sheltered child will know someone who has been a victim in some way. In Mildred Taylor's book *Roll of Thunder, Hear My*

Cry a discussion inevitably ensues as to whether Big Ma should have prepared Cassie for the racial injustices that existed in their town before Cassie became a victim. God knows it's easier to read about these things—abuse, alcohol and drugs, alienation, bullying, death and dying, eating disorders, poverty, prejudice, unwanted pregnancies, et cetera—than it is to experience them directly.

* * *

Teri Lesesne is past chair of NCTE's Standing Committee Against Censorship and a professor at Sam Houston State University. She is also the author of three professional books for teachers, *Reading Ladders, Naked Reading,* and *Making the Match,* as well as many articles on young adult literature. She is known to many teachers as the "Goddess of Young Adult Literature."

> **Question:** As author of several books that encourage wide reading, why do you argue that school libraries and individual classrooms need such a variety of young adult books? In English classes particularly, why isn't the canon of classics enough?

> **Answer:** There are a multitude of reasons why the canon is insufficient as a finite list of the books teens should read. Perhaps the overarching reason, though, is that *any* limit on reading, *any* narrowing of the curriculum, sends the message that books outside of the curriculum are not worthy enough for consideration *and* that the books included in the curriculum are somehow the ones that contain all of the information one will ever need.
>
> From a more pragmatic perspective, though, the canon does not contain literature that touches the lives of contemporary students. It is the literary equivalent of "When I was young . . ." Literature that connects with the lives, with the experiences, with the emotions, and with the needs of teens is the literature that will have the greatest impact.
>
> Finally, there is the ultimate question of how books come to be placed within this canon of literature. Is it possible that some books should be removed and others added in their stead? A list that never seems to change (and the research does indicate that the canon has remained relatively unchanged for decades, if not longer), a stagnant list, seems indefensible given that the time in which we live has changed considerably. It is important to remember that all of the

authors of canonical works were the *contemporary* authors of their time. And so I argue that the "list" needs to reflect contemporary authors as well as those classic works that still touch on the lives of our students.

*   *   *

David Moshman is professor of Educational Psychology, University of Nebraska at Lincoln and author of several articles and books including *Liberty & Learning: Academic Freedom for Teachers and Students* (2009).

> **Question:** In your book *Liberty & Learning: Academic Freedom for Teachers and Students*, you argue that academic freedom is intellectual freedom in academic contexts. What does this mean in practical terms for teachers who resist challenges to books in their curriculum or censorship of books on library or classroom shelves?

> **Answer:** Suppose you are a teacher whose choice of books has been challenged. How should you respond?
>
> First, you should consider whether the challenge is valid, at least in part. If you made a mistake, make a correction.
>
> But let's assume you believed you were making good choices on legitimate academic grounds and continue to believe that your choices were reasonable. In that case, it is not sufficient to defend the quality of the books. You must defend the selection process that led to their inclusion and explain the problem of permitting their removal.
>
> To do that you must explain the value of intellectual freedom in education in a way that will be convincing to your critics, or at least to administrators with the power to act on their behalf. You should start with the premise, shared by your critics and supervisors, that the purpose of education is to promote the learning and development of students, not the rights of teachers.
>
> But how do we promote the learning and development of students? There is no simple distinction between books that do this and books that don't. So who should decide what students read?
>
> One possibility is to let students decide. This is surely part of the answer. Students should do substantial additional reading beyond whatever we require, and should be free to make choices of their own. Autonomous action and free access to ideas are central to learning and development. Students should make decisions about what they read.
>
> But education is not just freedom to choose or freedom to read. Education involves a curriculum formulated by educators on the

basis of academic considerations. Books assigned or made available to students should be selected by teachers and other experts on the basis of academic criteria related to the topic at hand and the needs of students.

The freedom of teachers to make such academic decisions is academic freedom. Moreover, the free access of students to the books their teachers choose is also academic freedom, as is their freedom to disagree with whatever ideas they encounter in the books their teachers assign or otherwise make available.

Academic freedom, in other words, is intellectual freedom in academic contexts. Thus defined, academic freedom is crucial for students and teachers at all levels of education.

And what about administrators? The role of administrators with respect to curriculum is to protect academic freedom. This does not mean protecting the right of teachers to do as they please, nor does it mean defending the merit of every book that gets attacked. It means protecting the academic relationship of teacher and student by protecting, among other things, their joint choices of books to read.

Administrators, then, should respond to external pressures on academic choices by explaining why we are all best served by a system that protects intellectual freedom in education. You can help them explain this by helping them understand it.

But wouldn't it be more practical, at least in a public school, just to warn potential censors, including administrators, that removal of books would violate your First Amendment rights and those of your students? Wouldn't the threat of a lawsuit get more attention than a subtle argument about the nature and importance of academic freedom?

Unfortunately, under current law, such a lawsuit is no threat. The First Amendment, as interpreted by the U.S. Supreme Court, does not apply to student or faculty expression within the curriculum (*Hazelwood v. Kuhlmeier*, 1988) or to public employees when they are doing their jobs (*Garcetti v. Ceballos*, 2006). Relying on the First Amendment to rescue your curriculum or school library is wishful thinking, not practicality.

Explaining academic freedom is hard work and will not always prevent books from being removed or banned. But it should always be the first response. A clear understanding of academic freedom as intellectual freedom in education may help provide convincing arguments for respecting the academic choices of teachers and students.

*   *   *

Fredonia Ray, instructional coach for English Language Arts and Social Studies as well as teacher in the International Baccalaureate Program at Valdosta High School, defended Barbara Kingsolver's novel *The Bean Trees* when it was censored in her district. She was a recipient of NCTE/SLATE's Intellectual Freedom Award.

> **Question:** You went through a very public and painful censorship battle when defending Barbara Kingsolver's novel *The Bean Trees* for use in your English classroom. Was the battle worth it? Would you do it again?

> **Answer:** At a high school open house in 2004, a zealous mother declared Barbara Kingsolver's *The Bean Trees* pornographic and expressed her desire to have the book removed from the school. The book is not pornographic, nor does it corrupt children and put them on a path to jail, as the righteous youth director from her church asserted before the fearful school board. We had been teaching the book with school board approval for seven years, without protest or incident. The book deserved to be defended, and my students' right to read it deserved to be defended. Though the process of defending free speech and the freedom to read changed my life dramatically, I would do it again.
>
> When the battle began, I naïvely thought that a commendable 24-year career as an English teacher at my alma mater meant that my voice would be heard, if not respected.
>
> As time passed and the public weighed in on both sides, I took the position of a professional waiting for my professional superiors to defend the work of teachers and the right of students to read. When it became clear that would not happen, I wrote a series of three letters to the school board, pleading for their support. Instead, I received a reprimand from the superintendent, warning me to cease and desist or risk being charged with insubordination.
>
> With the support of NCTE and my union, Georgia Association of Educators, I maintained a firm, public position, and I would do so again for several reasons. The ordeal introduced me to an extraordinary extended community of former students, colleagues near and far, parents, the local newspaper, reasonable communities of faith, and the local university, all working to spread good sense. The battle also convinced me to seek employment elsewhere, and I

discovered a healthier world of support for teachers and teaching, readers and reading. I invited Barbara Kingsolver into the fray, and she responded to my letter with encouraging words for anyone hesitant to stand for something: "On the whole, over the decades, I do believe in a general reliable progress. We are making slow, permanent progress toward embracing broader truths and behaving more bravely as a country." I am happy to have made a contribution to that braver country!

Censorship Quotations to Prompt Thinking and Discussion

[Taken from GoodReads—www.goodreads.com/quotes/tag/censorship]

What is freedom of expression? Without the freedom to offend, it ceases to exist.

—Salman Rushdie

There are worse crimes than burning books. One of them is not reading them.

—Joseph Brodsky

Once a government is committed to the principle of silencing the voice of opposition, it has only one way to go, and that is down the path of increasingly repressive measures, until it becomes a source of terror to all its citizens and creates a country where everyone lives in fear.

—Harry S. Truman

It's not just the books under fire now that worry me. It is the books that will never be written. The books that will never be read. And all due to the fear of censorship. As always, young readers will be the real losers.

—Judy Blume

Torch every book.
Burn every page.
Char every word to ash.
Ideas are incombustible.
And therein lies your real fear.

—Ellen Hopkins

Books can not be killed by fire. People die, but books never die. No man and no force can abolish memory. . . . In this war, we know, books are weapons. And it is a part of your dedication always to make them weapons for man's freedom.

—Franklin D. Roosevelt

The real heroes are the librarians and teachers who at no small risk to themselves refuse to lie down and play dead for censors.

—Bruce Coville

We change people through conversation, not through censorship.

—Jay-Z, *Decoded*

Books That Deal with Censorship for Use with Students or Communities

And Tango Makes Three, Justin Richardson & Peter Parnell (2005)

> No discussion of censorship would be complete without considering this picture book that has been challenged and banned many times. The true story of a penguin with two daddies illuminates the censorship crisis in this country.

The Boy Who Dared, Susan Campbell Bartoletti (2008)

> This novel, based on true events, takes place during the Holocaust when a young boy targeted to be a Hitler Youth discovers books that are censored. This discovery and the boy's response to it will lead students into a deep and full discussion of censorship.

The Chosen One: A Novel, Carol Lynch Williams (2010)

> The female protagonist lives in an isolated polygamist cult, and her only escape is through books. When she is denied the opportunity to visit the mobile book library, she must decide how important books are to her. This book for mature readers will help them realize how fortunate they are to have ready access to the books they love.

Dear Author: Letters of Hope, Joan F. Kaywell (2007)

> This book contains a compilation of letters from teen readers to young adult authors, along with their replies. Young readers reached out to authors because the issues they address in their books or through their characters literally changed their lives.

Feed, M. T. Anderson (2002)

> This novel for mature readers, often compared to *Brave New World,* is set in a futuristic society where individual's brains are "fed" from the Internet. Could this be the end of a free-thinking society? There is much to discuss in this disturbing novel.

Places I Never Meant to Be: Original Stories by Censored Writers, Judy Blume (1999)

> Blume's introduction to this collection contains a powerful message about censorship and its tragic consequences. Students will enjoy reading the stories and researching why these authors have been censored.

The Sledding Hill, Chris Crutcher (2005)

> This clever and entertaining novel attacks censorship on all fronts. The protagonist turns into a freedom fighter over his favorite book, *Warren Peace,* and learns a lot about life in the process.

Court Decisions Regarding Intellectual Freedom/Censorship in Schools

Case/Date	Issue(s)	Ruling
Tinker v. the Des Moines [Iowa] School District—1969	Three students who wore black armbands to school as a symbol of their opposition to the war in Vietnam were suspended, despite any evidence that their actions were disruptive in any way.	The court ruled in favor of the plaintiffs, on the grounds that students do not "shed their constitutional rights to freedom of speech or expression at the schoolhouse gate." [See tinyurl.com/dxvhyc4 for 2007 interview with plaintiff Mary Beth Tinker.]
Presidents Council, District 25 v. Community School Board No. 25—1972	School board restricted students' access to Piri Thomas's *Down These Mean Streets*, which chronicles the author's challenges as he grew up in Spanish Harlem.	U.S. Supreme Court upheld school board's right to oversee book selection and dismissed the relevance of the First Amendment.
Minarcini v. Strongsville [Ohio] City School District—1977	The Strongsville City Board of Education rejected faculty recommendations to purchase Joseph Heller's *Catch-22* and Kurt Vonnegut's *God Bless You, Mr. Rosewater* and ordered the removal of *Catch-22* and Vonnegut's *Cat's Cradle* from the library.	The U.S. Court of Appeals for the Sixth Circuit ruled against the School Board, upholding students' First Amendment right to receive information and the librarian's right to disseminate it.
Right to Read Defense Committee of Chelsea v. School Committee of the City of Chelsea—1973	When the School Committee in Chelsea banned a poetry anthology, *Male and Female Under 18*, from the school library because they objected to a poem they found offensive, concerned citizens challenged the action in U.S. District Court.	In his ruling overturning the ban of the anthology, Judge Joseph L. Tauro wrote, "The library is 'a mighty resource in the marketplace of ideas.' There a student can literally explore the unknown, and discover areas of interest and thought not covered by the prescribed curriculum. The student who discovers the magic of

Case/Date	Issue(s)	Ruling
Right to Read Defense Committee of Chelsea v. School Committee of the City of Chelsea—1973 *(continued)*		the library is on the way to a life-long experience of self-education and enrichment. That student learns that a library is a place to test or expand upon ideas presented to him, in or out of the classroom. The most effective antidote to the poison of mindless orthodoxy is ready access to a broad sweep of ideas and philosophies. There is no danger from such exposure. The danger is mind control."
Board of Education, Island Trees Union Free School District no. 26 v. Pico—1982	A conservative community group, Parents of New York United, filed a complaint against a number of books in the school library that they found objectionable. The titles included *Slaughterhouse Five* by Kurt Vonnegut, Jr., *The Naked Ape* by Desmond Morris, *Down These Mean Streets* by Piri Thomas, *Best Short Stories of Negro Writers* (edited by Langston Hughes), *Laughing Boy* by Oliver LaFarge, *Go Ask Alice* (anonymous authorship), *Black Boy* by Richard Wright, *A Hero Ain't Nothing But a Sandwich* by Alice Childress, and *Soul on Ice* by Eldridge Cleaver.	Justice Brennan declared in the plurality opinion: "Local school boards may not remove books from school library shelves simply because they dislike the ideas contained in those books and seek by their removal to prescribe what shall be orthodox in politics, nationalism, religion, or other matters of opinion." See also Chris Crutcher's "Five Teens Win the Right to Read: Island Trees School District vs. Pico" at http://www.chriscrutcher.com/teens-can-stop-censors.html
Bethel School District v. Fraser—1986	Does the First Amendment prevent a school district from disciplining a high school student for giving a lewd speech at a high school assembly? In a speech filled with innuendo and sexual references, Mathew Fraser, a senior at Bethel High School in Bethel, Washington, nominated a classmate for a student government office. Although Fraser's candidate was overwhelmingly elected, Fraser was suspended from the school for three days and declared ineligible to speak at graduation. (Fraser was second in his class at that time.)	Mathew Fraser's parents appealed the school's disciplinary action. The Washington Supreme Court agreed that his free speech rights had been violated. The school board then appealed the case to the U.S. Supreme Court. By a 7–2 majority, the Court overturned the lower court's decision and supported the school district's action in disciplining Mathew Fraser.

Case/Date	Issue(s)	Ruling
Smith v. Board of School Commissioners of Mobile County, Alabama—1987	Parents and other citizen complainants contended that 44 textbooks adopted for use in the public school system promoted secular humanism and inhibited theistic religion.	The state circuit court ruled in favor of the plaintiffs, but on appeal, the Alabama Supreme Court, by a 7-2 margin, upheld the school officials' decisions to keep the challenged textbooks in the system.
Hazelwood School District v. Kuhlmeier—1988	Former high school students who were staff members of the school newspaper filed suit in federal court against school officials who had censored two stories—one that addressed students' experiences with pregnancy and another that dealt with the impact of divorce.	Although a U.S. Court of Appeals upheld the rights of the student journalists, on Jan. 13, 1988, the U.S. Supreme Court voted 5-3 to reverse the decision. The Court ruled that the Principal had the right to censor articles in the student newspaper that were deemed contrary to the school's educational mission. An online lesson plan for exploring the Hazelwood case and its ramifications is available at http://tinyurl.com/6wabo3o
Virgil v. School Board of Columbia County, Florida—1989	The Virgil case involves a Florida school board's decision to ban a high school literature text book because it contained selections from Aristophanes' play *Lysistrata* and Geoffrey Chaucer's "The Miller's Tale."	The U.S. Court of Appeals for the 11th district ruled only that the Board's removal of the two works from the curriculum did not violate the Constitution, making a point not to endorse the Board's decision. The Court wrote, "Like the district court, we seriously question how young persons just below the age of majority can be harmed by these masterpieces of Western literature. However, having concluded that there is no constitutional violation, our role is not to second guess the wisdom of the Board's action."
Monteiro v. Tempe Union High School District—1989	Kathy Monteiro, the mother of a student (referred to as "Jane Doe") in a freshman English class, objected to two literary classics assigned in her daughter's English class: Twain's *The Adventures of Huckleberry Finn* and "A Rose for Emily," a William Faulkner short story. The parent alleged that each of these literary works "contains repeated use of the profane, insulting and racially derogatory term 'nigger.'" The complaint contended that Jane	The U.S. Court of Appeals, Ninth circuit, issued such a clear, accessible, and persuasive ruling in this case that we're including a substantial portion of their findings: "Here we consider whether the school board's interest in exercising its broad discretion in assigning the literary works in question and the students' First Amendment interest in reading those works are collectively outweighed by the constitutional and statutory interests of students who assert that they are injured by the mandatory assignments.

Case/Date	Issue(s)	Ruling
Monteiro v. Tempe Union High School District—1989 *(continued)*	Doe and other African American students suffered psychological injuries as a result of these works being assigned reading.	To resolve this controversy, we must consider whether the assignment of material deemed to have educational value by school authorities may in itself serve as the basis for an injunction by a court or an award of damages, when the challenge to the material is founded on its message or the language it employs. In other words, may courts ban books or other literary works from school curricula on the basis of their content? We answer that question in the negative, even when the works are accused of being racist in whole or in part. To begin with, Monteiro's amended complaint—and other lawsuits threatening to attach civil liability on the basis of the assignment of a book—would severely restrict a student's right to receive material that his school board or other educational authority determines to be of legitimate educational value. The amended complaint requests, under the threat of civil liability, that the school remove the literary works from the classroom. Certainly when a school board identifies information that it believes to be a useful part of a student's education, that student has the right to receive the information. Indeed, the Eighth Circuit has concluded that a school board's removal of material from the classroom curriculum solely on the basis of its message has a powerful symbolic effect on a student or teacher's First Amendment rights—despite the material's availability in the library—and is, therefore, unconstitutional. See http://caselaw.findlaw.com/us-9th-circuit/1281281.html for more compelling discussion of the ruling in this case.

Case/Date	Issue(s)	Ruling
Counts v. Cedarville School District—2003	The school board of the Cedarville, Arkansas, school district voted to restrict students' access to the Harry Potter books, on the grounds that the books promoted disobedience and disrespect for authority and dealt with witchcraft and the occult. Students in the district were then required to obtain a signed permission slip from their parents or guardians before they would be allowed to borrow any of the Harry Potter books from school libraries.	The District Court overturned the Board's decision and ordered the books returned to unrestricted circulation, on the grounds that the restrictions violated students' First Amendment right to read and receive information.
Gillman v. Holmes County School District, U.S. District Court, Northern District of Florida, Panama City Division—2008	Heather Gillman, a junior at Ponce de Leon High School in the Florida Panhandle, was forbidden by her principal to wear any sort of clothing, stickers, buttons, or symbols to show her support of equal rights for gay people. Gillman and other students were showing solidarity for a gay friend who was being harassed at school. With the support of the ACLU of Florida (which provided counsel and representation) and her mother, Gillman sued the school board in her district.	After a one-day trial, on July 24, 2008, United States Judge Richard Smoak ruled that the "School Board for Holmes County, Florida, has (1) violated Plaintiff's right to free speech and (2) discriminated against her viewpoint, in violation of the First and Fourteenth Amendments to the United States Constitution." See http://tinyurl.com/7v3kv5d for more information about this case, including a short video featuring the student plaintiff.

National Organizations That Offer Support and Resources for Challenges and Censorship

The American Booksellers Foundation for Free Expression—www.abffe.com

ABFFE is a national community of booksellers that opposes efforts to ban books in public schools and libraries. They also will file amicus briefs in cases challenging school censorship.

The American Civil Liberties Union—www.aclu.org

The ACLU works daily in courts, legislatures, and communities to defend and preserve individual rights and liberties, such as freedom of speech, press, religion, and unlawful discrimination.

The American Library Association's Office for Intellectual Freedom—www.ala.org/offices/oif

The Office for Intellectual Freedom is dedicated to free access to libraries and library materials. They offer webinars, meetings, and information, and equip attorneys to counsel and defend libraries and librarians. This office also sponsors Banned Books Weeks.

The Freedom Forum—www.freedomforum.org

The Freedom Forum is a nonpartisan foundation that "champions the First Amendment as a cornerstone of democracy." The center sponsors a website on the First Amendment, firstamendmentcenter.org, which features daily updates on news about First Amendment related issues.

The Freedom to Read Foundation—www.ftrf.org

The Freedom to Read Foundation, affiliated with the American Library Association, protects, promotes, and defends the First Amendment, specifically in libraries. They will participate directly in litigation. Their quarterly newsletter is a benefit of membership in the FTRF.

National Coalition Against Censorship—www.ncac.org

NCAC promotes freedom of thought, inquiry, and expression and opposes censorship in all its forms. The organization offers direct assistance and counseling to anyone confronted with censorship and serves as a clearinghouse of information. The coalition unites over 50 organizations dedicated to promoting free expression.

The National Council of Teachers of English Anti-Censorship Center—www.ncte.org/action/anti-censorship

> NCTE offers guidelines, procedures, advice, and vigorous support to teachers faced with challenges to texts (e.g., literary works, films and videos, drama productions) or teaching methods used in their classrooms and schools. They also provide rationales for teaching challenged books.

People for the American Way—www.pfaw.org

> People for the American Way promotes freedom of expression and works against censorship in all its forms.

References

Alexie, S. (2008). *Absolutely true diary of a part-time Indian.* Waterville, ME: Thorndike Press.

Allington, R. (2002). You can't learn much from books you can't read. *Educational Leadership, 60*(3), 16–19.

Allington, R. (2011). *What really matters to struggling readers: Designing research-based programs* (3rd ed.). Boston, MA: Pearson Education.

Allington, R. L., & Gabriel, R. E. (2012). Every child, every day. *Educational Leadership, 69*(6), 10–15.

Anderson, L. H. (2000). *Speak.* Carmel, CA: Hampton-Brown.

Anderson, R. C., Wilson, P. T., & Fielding, L. G. (1988). Growth in reading and how children spend their time outside of school. *Reading Research Quarterly, 23,* 285–303.

Atwell, N. (2007). *The reading zone: How to help kids become skilled, passionate, habitual, critical readers.* New York: Scholastic.

Baca, J. S. (2010). *Stories from the edge.* Portsmouth, NH: Heinemann.

Beers, K. (2003). *When kids can't read, what teachers can do: A guide for teachers, 6–12.* Portsmouth, NH: Heinemann.

Blume, J. [n.d.]. About censorship . . . in her own words. Available at http://www.randomhouse.com/highschool/RHI_magazine/pdf3/Blume.pdf

Brooks, G. (2011). *Caleb's crossing.* New York: Viking.

Brown, J. E. (2000). Creating a censorship simulation. *The ALAN Review, 27*(3), 27–30. Available at http://scholar.lib.vt.edu/ejournals/ALAN/spring00/brownres.html

Burress, L., Karolides, N. J., & Kean, J. M. (2001). *Censored books: Critical viewpoints.* Lanham, MD: Scarecrow Press.

Calkins, L., Ehrenworth, M., & Lehman, C. (2012). *Pathways to the Common Core: Accelerating achievement.* Portsmouth, NH: Heinemann.

Cambourne, B. (1995, November). Toward an educationally relevant theory of literacy learning: Twenty years of inquiry. *The Reading Teacher, 49,* 182–190.

Carlson, P. (1987, January 4). Banning books in the schools: When teachers and fundamentalists clash, children get burned. *The Washington Post Magazine,* pp. 10–17, 40–41.

Coleman, D., & Pimentel, S. (2011). Publishers' criteria for the common core state standards in English language arts and Literacy, Grades 3–12. Available at http://www.corestandards.org/assets/Publishers_Criteria_for_3-12.pdf

Collins, C. (1986, June 6). Your child's textbooks: Have you read them? *The News Herald* [Panama City, FL], p. 11.

Collins, S. (2008). *The hunger games.* New York: Scholastic.

Conroy, P. (2010). *My reading life.* New York: Nan A. Talese/Doubleday.

Cormier, R. (1979). *After the first death.* New York: Pantheon Books.

Cormier, R. (1988). *Fade.* New York: Delacorte.

Cormier, R. (2007). *I am the cheese*. New York: Knopf Books for Young Readers.

Dahl, R. (2011). *James and the giant peach*. New York: Penguin Books.

Donelson, K. (1979, February). Censorship in the 1970s: Some ways to handle it when it comes (and it will). *English Journal,* p. 47.

Ferlazzo, L. (2012). Response: Ways to help our students become better readers. Available at http://blogs.edweek.org/teachers/classroom_qa_with_larry_ferlazzo/2012/02/response_ways_to_help_our_students_become_better_readers.html

Green, J. (2005). *Looking for Alaska*. New York: Dutton Children's Books.

Guthrie, J. T. (Ed.). (2008). *Engaging adolescents in reading*. Thousand Oaks, CA: Corwin Press.

Harvey, S., & Daniels, H. (2009). *Comprehension & collaboration: Inquiry circles in action*. Portsmouth, NH: Heinemann.

Horne, K. [n.d.]. Believe in what you teach, down to the comma: What my experience with censorship taught me about trust, freedom and standing up for what you believe. Available at http://www.randomhouse.com/highschool/RHI_magazine/pdf3/Horne.pdf

Ivey, G. (2011). What not to read: A book intervention. *Voices from the Middle, 19*(2), 22–26.

Ivey, G., & Fisher, D. (2006). *Creating literacy-rich schools for adolescents*. Alexandria, VA: Association for Supervision and Curriculum Development.

Jenkins, C. A. (2008). Book challenges, challenging books, and young readers: The research picture. *Language Arts, 85*(3), 228–236.

Karolides, N. (Ed.). (2002). *Censored books II: Critical viewpoints, 1985–2002*. Lanham, MD: Scarecrow Press.

Krashen, S. D. (2004). *The power of reading : Insights from the research* (2nd ed.). Westport, CT: Libraries Unlimited; Portsmouth, NH: Heinemann.

Larsson, S. (2009). *The girl with the dragon tattoo*. New York: Vintage Crime/Black Lizard.

Lowry, L. (2011). *The giver*. Boston: Houghton Mifflin Books for Children.

McCann, C. (2009). *Let the great world spin: A novel*. New York: Random House.

Millay, E. S. V. (1988). *Collected sonnets*. New York: Harper & Row.

Moshman, D. (2009). *Liberty & learning: Academic freedom for teachers and students*. Portsmouth, NH: Heinemann.

Myracle, L. (2011). *Shine*. New York: Amulet Books.

Newkirk, T. (2012). How we really comprehend fiction. *Educational Leadership, 69*(6), 28–32.

Nilsen, A. P., & Donelson, K. L. (2009). *Literature for today's young adults* (8th ed.). Boston: Pearson.

Patchett, A. (2011). *State of wonder*. New York: HarperCollins.

Paton, A. (2003). *Cry the beloved country*. New York: Simon & Schuster.

Pfeffer, S. B. (1980). *About David*. New York: Delacorte.

Pilgreen, J. L. (2000). *How to organize and manage a sustained silent reading program*. Portsmouth, NH: Boynton-Cook.

Pipkin, G., & Lent, R. C. (2002). *At the schoolhouse gate: Lessons in intellectual freedom*. Portsmouth, NH: Heinemann.

Reid, L., with Neufeld, J. (Eds.). (1999). *Rationales for teaching young adult literature*. Portland, ME: Calendar Islands Publishers.

Rosenblatt, L. (1994). *The reader, the text, and the poem: The transactional theory of literacy work*. Carbondale: Southern Illinois University Press.

Routman, R. (2002). *Reading essentials: The specifics you need to teach reading well*. Portsmouth, NH: Heinemann.

Scales, P. (2010, August). Weighing in: Three bombs, two lips, and a martini glass. *Booklist*. Available at http://www.booklistonline.com/ProductInfo.aspx?pid=4341541&AspxA utoDetectCookieSupport=1

Sepetys, R. (2011). *Between shades of gray*. New York: Philomel Books.

Seuss, Dr. (1971). *The Lorax*. New York: Random House.

Stillman, A. (2010, September 15). The Absolutely True Diary. . . Absolutely Banned. *Cedar County Republican*.

Tovani, C. (2000). *I read it but I don't get it: Comprehension strategies for adolescent readers*. Portland, ME: Stenhouse.

Wiesenthal, S. (1998). *The sunflower: On the possibilities and limits of forgiveness*. New York: Schocken.

Wilde, O. (2001). *The happy prince and other tales*. Mineola, NY: Dover.

Wolfe, T. (1995). *Look homeward, angel: A story of the buried life*. New York : Scribner Paperback Fiction.

Index

About the Authors

ReLeah Cossett Lent, a former teacher, is now a full-time writer and consultant. Her latest book is *Overcoming Textbook Fatigue: 21st Century Tools to Reinvigorate Teaching and Learning* and her latest book with Teachers College Press is *Literacy for Real*. She has authored many books and articles about adolescent literacy and is currently chair of the National Council of Teachers of English's Standing Committee Against Censorship.

Gloria Pipkin, a former teacher, has written extensively about censorship and co-authored *At the Schoolhouse Gate: Lessons in Intellectual Freedom* and *Silent No More: Voices of Courage in American Schools* with ReLeah Cossett Lent.

Together, Gloria and ReLeah were honored with intellectual freedom awards from the National Council of Teachers of English as well as the American Library Association for "notable contributions to the cause of intellectual freedom" and for their "defense and advocacy of its principles." ReLeah was the recipient of the PEN/Newman's Own Intellectual Freedom Award in 1999.